RISE
to the
CHALLENGE
of
MINISTRY

Dr. Terrance Jenkins, Th.D,D.D.

PublishAmerica
Baltimore

First printing

At the specific preference of the author, PublishAmerica allowed this work to remain exactly as the author intended, verbatim, without editorial input.

ISBN: 1-4241-2401-8 (softcover)
ISBN: 978-1-4489-6655-4 (hardcover)
PUBLISHED BY PUBLISHAMERICA, LLLP
www.publishamerica.com
Baltimore

Printed in the United States of America

Dedicated to:

My precious wife, Julie, for her love and dedication to me over the years which has allowed me to spend time and energy studying the Word of God in preparation for ministry.

This book is also dedicated to those who are in ministry and those contemplating entering ministry, especially the pastoral ministry. My prayer is that you will be blessed, encouraged and strengthened in the Lord as you lead God's people to become all that they can be.

FOREWORD

Dr. Terrance Jenkins is a man I met some years ago, but have recently come to know him and his wife Julie, in a much more intimate way. We have shared some of the victories and yes, some of the frustrations of ministry as it regards the Pastoral field. When I met him again, recently, at a Conference for the Ontario Conference of the Pentecostal Holiness Church of Canada, he told me he was working on a book and would like me to read it over. I was more than happy to do this when he told me briefly, (He told me the title!), that his book had to do with THE CHLALLENGES OF MINISTRY.

I have been in ministry for forty six years as an associate Pastor, and Interim Pastor, Evangelist and for the past twenty years as full time Pastor. This book gives insights into ministry that I wish I could have read forty years ago. Those who are in ministry, and those contemplating entering ministry (especially Pastoral Ministry) really need to read this book!

Dr. Clarence Wood, Pastor
Pastoral Care, The Tabernacle
Sarnia, Ontario, Canada

PREFACE

The modern age is one of revolution—revolution motivated by insight into the enormous human suffering and need of one kind or another. Several advocates have given their point of view for a solution to the complexities of this problem which touches the fabric of humanity around the globe. Pleas for holiness, and attacks on sin and Satan, were used for ages as the guide and cure for the human situation. Amid the flood of techniques for self-fulfillment there is an epidemic of depression, personal emptiness, and escapism through drugs and alcohol, cultic obsession, consumerism, sex and violence. So, obviously, from the Christian perspective one must conclude that the problem is a spiritual one and much deeper than we are ready to accept.

I strongly believe that within the pages of this book, THE CHALLENGE OF MINISTRY, lies the solution that should shake us not only as Christian Ministers but also the aspiring young leader in the church. Dr. Terrance Jenkins has taken the time to diligently research and address the various topics in this book and I do hope that each of us would take a second look at our own commitment to the calling of God upon our lives.

Rev. M. S. Armoogam, B.C.M., C.P.C.
Campus Director
Canadian School of Christian Ministry
Toronto, Ontario, Canada

CONTENTS

INTRODUCTION
RISE TO THE CHALLENGE

I was asked to be the opening speaker for a week-long, city-wide crusade in the city of Edmonton, Alberta, Canada in 1992. The main speaker was coming from the Dominican Republic. The theme of the crusade was **"TAKING BACK WHAT THE DEVIL HAS STOLEN."**

I sought the Lord for the right message to present to the people for opening night. He impressed upon me the thought that has become the subject of this book, **"RISE TO THE CHALLENGE."** Then, as I questioned the Lord as to how to present such a message to the people so that they would fully understand what I was talking about, He directed my attention to the tiny nation of Israel.

First Samuel, chapter seventeen, gives us the story of a tiny, peace loving nation, called Israel, being challenged to battle by its enemy, the Philistines. They, like the enemy of the Church of Jesus Christ, not only challenged Israel, but also defied Israel's God.

The enemy can not do that and get away with it! He will pay the consequences of his actions.

Israel, like most of the church world of our day, was fearful of the enemy. In other words, why rock the boat?

Do not disturb the status quo. We don't want to anger the enemy. REALLY? When Goliath would come out and roar Israel would run from him and hide. That's all the devil can do—roar like a lion. Jesus Christ, our Commander-in-Chief is the Lion of the tribe of Judah. We need not run from the enemy. We need to run at him as David, the son of Jesse did, and slay the enemy. **RISE TO THE CHALLENGE**, run to meet it and conquer it in the name which is above every name, the name of Jesus.

The Church of Jesus Christ is a peace-loving organism, but when the devil challenges it by trying to tear it apart through lies, deceitfulness, lust, pride, discouragement, and the like, then the Church must **RISE TO THE CHALLENGE**—not only to keep what it has, but also to take back that which the devil has stolen from it. Amen!

God's people must never run from the enemy. Rather, they must run at him, and put him to flight. The Bible states "one would put a thousand to flight, and two would put ten thousand to flight" *(I like God's kind of multiplication, don't you?)*

God only asks that we RISE UP, take our stand against the enemy, with the whole armor of God on (Ephesians 6:10-17). Then, in submission to God (James 4:7), resist the devil and he will have no choice but to flee from us. Praise the Lord! We have the victory, RISE UP AND TAKE IT!!

You can be that person who will take a stand, and say, *"Here am I Lord. I will stand in the gap and make up the hedge for my loved ones or against this infirmity because you have promised me victory in this area."* Are you ready to **RISE TO THE CHALLENGE** for ministry to a hurting world?

These few words that I have written are based upon

the message that I mentioned above and even though the subjects are not written in depth, I trust that they shall be enough to stir your heart so that you will take up the mantle, rise to the challenge of ministry, allowing the Lord to use you in a way that will bring both spiritual and physical healing to the body of Christ, as well as, bring lost souls into the Kingdom of God. I believe that God is calling a new breed of preachers and workers into the harvest field in these last days who will be willing to take a stand against all the forces of the evil one so as to rescue the lost and dying. This new breed of workers will **RISE TO THE CHALLENGE** and will not back down from the enemy, but like the young teenager, David, will run to the enemy, confident that the Lord will bring deliverance. God will not fail His people!

Take courage, trust in the Lord, delight yourself in Him, and He will plant desires in your heart that He can bring to pass for you. There are many other areas of ministry besides the few that I have mentioned such as children's church, nursery, maintenance, altar workers, singers, worship leaders and so on. Whatever area of ministry God has called you to do, do it with all of your might. Whatever you do, do it as unto the Lord and He will bless you for it. Whatever your giant may be, face it in the name of Jesus and it will flee before you. **RISE TO THE CHALLENGE!** The victory is yours in Jesus' name!

CHAPTER ONE
THE CHALLENGE OF CHRISTIAN MINISTRY

World's Bible Dictionary states, "Christian ministry is a very broad subject and may be conveniently studied through looking at topics that deal with its various aspects. According to its most common biblical usage, **ministry** simply means **service**."

The Twentieth Century Bible Dictionary states that ministry is: "1) the act of ministering or serving as a minister of God (Acts 6:4; 12:25); 2) the office, position, or function of a minister as a servant of the Church, figuratively 'the body of Christ' (II Corinthians 4:1; Ephesians 4:12)."

PASTORAL MINISTRY:

Acts 20:28 states, "Be on guard for yourselves and for all the flock, among which the Holy Spirit has made you overseers, to shepherd (to feed) the Church of God which He purchased with His own blood" (NASB). God, through Christ had paid an awful price (His death) for this flock. Therefore, the admonition is not only to be on guard for oneself, but also for the souls of those who are under the minister's charge. What an awesome responsibility!

From Baker's Dictionary of Practical Theology we read, "Paul, the apostle, had given himself fully to the pastoral ministry at Ephesus, for three years, with many tears, trials and lowliness of mind. His concern was not for himself but for the flock over which God had placed him. Acts 20:19-21 says, "Serving the Lord with all humility of mind, and with many tears, and temptations (trials), which befell me by the lying in wait (plotting) of the Jews: and how I kept back nothing that was profitable unto you but have showed you, and have taught you publicly, and from house to house, testifying both to the Jews, and also to the Greeks, repentance toward God, and faith toward our Lord Jesus Christ." He had set himself as an example for the Ephesian elders to follow. That example is still sufficient for us as Christian ministers today.

One can hardly understand the personal relationship which must exist between the pastor and his people unless he recalls the relationship between a shepherd and his sheep. Jesus, Himself, drew upon this fact to relate His own relationship with His sheep (John 10:3-5). A shepherd gave individual names to his sheep. He did not simply know them collectively, but individually. Verse three says, "He calleth His own sheep by name, and leadeth them out." He may not know the sheep of another flock by name but he knew his own. Furthermore, his sheep knew his voice and would not follow another shepherd. At night many flocks shared the same fold. In the morning a given shepherd would give a certain call. His sheep, recognizing his voice, followed him as he led them (v.4). He did not drive them—he led them, and because they knew his voice, they followed him."

What a blessing when this kind of relationship exists between pastor and congregation! However, this relationship does not just happen—it comes about as a result of the pastor living with his flock, knowing their needs, and sharing their problems. A preacher can only, effectively, preach to his congregation on Sunday, after he has lived with them and shared himself with them throughout the week. However, IF A PASTOR IS TO FEED HIS FLOCK, HE MUST BE FED. He must study the Word (II Timothy 2:15), so as to be able to adequately cut through it and feed the flock. It is a difficult thing to strike the delicate balance between study time and ministration time. But that balance must be maintained if the shepherd is to properly fulfill his ministry. Many times the sheep do not follow the shepherd in some worthy program because they do not know him. John 10:5 says, "A stranger they will not follow, but will flee from him: for they know not the voice of strangers."

As shepherds, the Ephesian elders were to feed or tend the flocks. Feeding the flock involves the teaching and preaching ministry of the pastor. Tending the flock encompasses a multitude of pastoral duties wherein the pastor identifies himself with the many needs of his people. He must be a comforter, healer, worshiper, reconciler, and the list goes on. He cannot be indifferent to any of these. He must have a heart of compassion and tenderness to meet every situation that arises among his flock.

The pastor must both console and rebuke with tears. He must lift up the hands which hang down, strengthen the feeble knees; and make straight paths for the flock. Hebrews 12:12, 13, "Wherefore lift up (strengthen) the hands which hang down, and the feeble knees; and make straight paths for your feet lest that which is lame be turned out of the way; but let it rather be healed." He must reclaim the wandering sheep. He must rejoice with those who do rejoice, and weep with those who weep. He must become all things to all men as he seeks to lead them to Christ, and to enable them to walk in His will and way.

The pastor is to become one with the flock, apart from their sins, so as to lead them "into the unity of the faith, and of the full knowledge of the Son of God, into a mature man, unto the measure of the stature of the fullness of Christ" (Ephesians 4: 13). The pastor is to protect his flock against grievous wolves that would enter in to destroy them (Acts 20:29).

The pastor is to guard his flock against the blatant forces of evil which openly challenge the church and its ministry. He is also to guard against wolves in sheep clothing who would attempt to lead the sheep away under the guise of a supposedly more advanced theology. The pastor must "contend for the faith" (Jude 3), "speaking the truth in love" (Ephesians 4:15). This constant feeding and tending the flock will enable it to stand against every "contrary wind of doctrine" (Ephesians 4: 14).

Jesus said, "I am the good Shepherd: the good Shepherd is willing to give His life for His sheep." (John 10:11). Indeed, THIS IS THE TEST OF A GOOD SHEPHERD—**how far he will go to protect his flock.** The 'hireling' will not stand in times of adversity, but will flee, leaving the flock alone to fight the wolves that come among them. The GOOD SHEPHERD will stand against all odds to protect and care for the flock that has been entrusted to his care. He will not run from the wolves of false doctrine and spiritual or physical illnesses. Rather, he will take the **'Sword of the Spirit'** and fight off everything that comes to do his flock harm. THE CHALLENGE OF MINISTRY IS TRULY AN AWESOME RESPONSIBILITY!

The true pastor must be willing to give his life in complete dedication to his calling.

Discouragement or selfishness cannot have any place in THE CHALLENGE OF MINISTRY because the flock must be put above one's own agenda and plans. The pastor must remain faithful to his calling. This really is the point in Paul's word to the Ephesian elders in Acts 20:34 where he quoted the words of the Lord, "It is more blessed to give than to receive." The last beatitude of Jesus, often quoted in support of faithful stewardship of one's possession, more correctly relates to the stewardship of a pastor with respect to his calling.

A final note on the study of PASTORAL MINISTRY with reference to Psalm 23, "The Lord is my Shepherd." David had been a shepherd and knew the pastoral duties of such. In this Psalm he transferred these ministries to the care for him on the part of the Great Shepherd. The pastor will do well to parallel his ministry as an under-shepherd according to Jehovah's Shepherd care for His own. A reading of this great Psalm in this light will truly enhance the ministerial responsibility of the pastor. When it is interpreted in light of the life of Jesus—His compassion, love, faithfulness, and sacrifice—it calls for a re-consecration of every pastor to the opportunity which God in Christ has given to him. He is reminded afresh that the Holy Spirit has made him overseer "to all the flock."

CHAPTER TWO
THE CHALLENGE OF BODY MINISTRY

No member of the BODY OF CHRIST is unimportant or unnecessary. As the natural body consists of many members, so also, the Body of Christ is made up of many members—Christ being the Head.

First Corinthians 12:21, 22 and 25 states, "And the eye cannot say unto the hand, I have no need of thee: nor again the head to the feet, I have no need of you. Nay, much more those members of the body, which seem to be more feeble (weak), are necessary: and those members of the body, which we think to be less honorable, upon these we bestow more abundant honor; and our uncomely (unpresentable) parts have more abundant comeliness (modesty). That there should be no schism in the body; but that the members should have the same care one for another."

Dr. F. F. Bruce, commenting on the foregone passage, remarks: "No member is less a part of the body than any other member: all are necessary. Variety of organs, limbs, and functions is of the essence of bodily life. No organ could establish a monopoly in the body by taking over the functions of the others. A body consisting of a single organ would be a monstrosity."

Matthew Henry, on this subject states, "Variety in the members of the body contributes to its beauty. So it is for the beauty and good appearance of the Church that there should be a diversity of gifts. We should be doing the duties of our own place, and not quarreling with the others, that we are not in theirs. All the members of the body are useful and necessary to each other. Every member serves some good purpose or other. Nor is there a member of the body of Christ but ought to be useful to his fellow-members, and in some cases, is needful to them. Those who excel in any gift cannot say that they have no need of those who in that gift are their inferiors, while perhaps, in other gifts, they exceed them. The eye has need of the hand, and the head of the feet. Divine wisdom has ordered things in this manner that the members of the body should not be schismatic. The members of the natural body are made to have a care and concern for each other. **So should it be in Christ's body.** CHRISTIAN SYMPATHY IS A GREAT BRANCH OF CHRISTIAN DUTY."

In speaking of this subject of **'body ministry'** the writers of a book entitled, FOUNDATIONS OF PENTECOSTAL THEOLOGY, conclude that, "the concept of the church as the BODY OF CHRIST has been given new emphasis in recent years. This new emphasis has led to important insights for worship and ministry. Too often ministry has been viewed as coming exclusively from a rostrum or pulpit and only by designated clergy. When ministry is so conceived, the members of the congregation become merely spectators, whose only activity is that of filling the pews. The Bible picture of **body life** does not support such a limited view of ministry. God has, indeed, placed spiritual leadership in the Church to preach and teach; but the object of their preaching, teaching, and pastoral care is that of perfecting or equipping the saints to minister one to another and to the world."

Ephesians 4:11-15 (NASB), "And He gave some as apostles, and some as prophets, and some as evangelists, and some as pastors and teachers, for the equipping of the saints for the work of service, to the building up of the body of Christ; until we all attain to the unity of the faith, and of the knowledge of the Son of God, to a mature man, to the measure of the stature which belongs to the fullness of Christ. As a result, we are no longer to be children....; but speaking the truth in love, we are to grow up in all aspects into Him, Who is the Head, even Christ."

The writers of this book go on to state: "From this concept of body ministry as expressed by the Apostle Paul, several facts are clear: **First,** it is the Lord's intention that every member of the body of Christ have a ministry. Every member of a human body contributes to the preservation, growth, health and activity of that body; if some members do not function, disease results. Many of the ills of the Church have been the result of a non-functioning membership. To achieve total participation in the work and worship of the church, God has provided spiritual leadership to equip and mature the saints, and the gifts of the Spirit to empower and give direction to them.

Second, the central purpose of body ministry is that of the edification of the whole church. The test of the value and validity of body ministry, and of the exercise of the gifts, is in whether they edify the body of Christ. Peter wrote, "As every man has received the gift even so minister the same one to another, as good stewards of the manifold grace of God" (1 Peter 4:10). Ministry and gifts are truly a stewardship. The believer's gift is not given primarily for his edification; it is a stewardship for others, for the church family.

Third, when the whole body ministers in unity and love, the result is spiritual and numerical growth. "From whom the whole body, being fitted and held together by that which every joint supplies, according to the proper working of each individual part, causes the growth of the body for the building up of itself in love" (Ephesians 4:16, NASB). In these days much is said of church growth. Optimum growth of the church cannot be accomplished by the efforts of church leaders, pastors, evangelists, missionaries, etc. Ideal growth results only when the entire church ministers. Therefore, **'every member a minister'** ought to become the benchmark of every local congregation. Only as each member becomes a minister can the church have an effective 'BODY MINISTRY' within itself and to the world to reach them with the gospel of Jesus Christ.

Fourth, when the whole church ministers, there must be present the adhesive force of love, **the agape love of God.** Unless total church participation is motivated by, and carried out in, a spirit of love and submission to the leadership the growth accomplished may be transient and the ministry performed may be less than edifying. The Scriptures teach: "Seeing you have purified your souls in obeying the truth through the Spirit in unfeigned love of the brethren, love one another fervently with a pure heart" (1 Peter 1:22). Jesus also stated, "By this shall all men know that ye are my disciples, if ye have **love one for another**" (John 13:35).

CHAPTER THREE
THE CHALLENGE OF PREACHING

Romans 10:14, 15, "How then shall they call on Him in Whom they have not believed? And how shall they believe in Him of Whom they have not heard? And how shall they hear without a preacher? And how shall they preach, except they be sent? As it is written, How beautiful are the feet of them that preach the gospel of peace, and bring glad tidings of good things."

G. Jeffreys Williamson declares, "All truly great preachers can trace their greatness to the anointing of the Holy Spirit as the source of their knowledge, the potency of their powers, and the fluency of their speech."

The great C. H. Spurgeon stated, "We are, in a certain sense, our own tools, and therefore must keep ourselves in order. If I want to preach the gospel I can only use my own voice, therefore I must train my vocal powers. I can only think with my own brain, and feel with my own heart, therefore I must educate my intellectual and emotional faculties."

One more quote worthy of attention at this time is from Samuel Chadwick, who said, "I have loved my job with a passionate and consuming love. I would rather preach than do anything else I know in this world. I would rather preach than eat my dinner, or have a holiday. It has its price in agony of sweat and tears, and no calling has such joys and heart-breaks, but it is a calling an archangel might covet, and I thank God that of His grace He called me into this ministry."

That statement by Rev. Chadwick is one which depicts the passion and all consuming love that one must have to be successful in ministry. For many years my vacation would involve preaching in other churches because I love to preach the gospel so much. It is my very life. Take anything else away from me but don't take the ministry of preaching away. It is such a challenge and yet such an awesome responsibility because every word that is spoken will affect the hearer in some way for eternity.

The **Greek** word for preacher in the New Testament is **KERUX,** meaning herald. The **Grimm-Thayer lexicon** defines it: "A messenger vested with public authority, who conveyed the official messages of kings or magistrates ....."

Mr. W. E. Vine states, **"KERUX** indicates the preacher as giving the proclamation; EVANGELISTES points to his message as glad tidings; APOSTOLOS suggests his relationship to Him by Whom he is sent."

Jesus, quoting from the Old Testament prophet, Isaiah, said, "The Spirit of the Lord is upon me (why) because He hath anointed me to PREACH the gospel to the poor; He hath sent me to heal the broken hearted, to PREACH deliverance to the captives, and recovering of sight to the blind, to set at liberty them that are bruised. To PREACH the acceptable year of the Lord," (Luke 4:18, 19).

Therefore, we find that true preachers are not so much men who speak a message on God's behalf, but men through whom God speaks and delivers His message of hope, love, joy, peace, etc. They are not necessarily men who operate in the gifts, but men who allow the Spirit to flow through them with spiritual manifestation of the gifts.

World's Bible Dictionary says, "The Bible often mentions preaching and teaching together, for the two are closely related. It seems at times there is little difference between them. The same person was usually both a preacher and a teacher" (Matthew 4:23; 11:1; Acts 5:42, etc.). In my book "Nineteen Special Gifts of God to His Children" I wrote one complete chapter on the subject of 'pastors and teachers' in which I stated that "ALL PASTORS MUST BE TEACHERS BUT NOT ALL TEACHERS ARE PASTORS." One is not a true pastor unless he can teach the Word of God so that his flock can understand what the Word has to say for their life today, and then apply that which they have heard.

Sometimes preaching is proclamation, such as in announcing the **good news of the gospel** to those who need it, while teaching is more concerned with the instruction of those who already believe the gospel message. Teaching is necessary also for those who do not believe, while preaching the great facts of the Gospel of Jesus Christ is still necessary to challenge the believer.

To preach the gospel is to preach Christ. God's message for believers and non-believers centers in Him. The gospel is more than just a message of salvation; it is the whole new life in Jesus Christ. II Corinthians 5:17 says, "Therefore if any man be in Christ, he is a new creature (creation): old things are passed away; behold, all things are become new."

God wants mankind to learn about Him, to know Him personally, and to be instructed in what He desires for them. He has, therefore, revealed Himself to man; He has spoken to man. He has done this dramatically through His Son, Jesus Christ, but He has also given a written revelation through the Scriptures. Note the words of John 1:1 and 14, "In the beginning was the Word, and the Word was with God, and the Word was God. And the Word was made (became) flesh, and dwelt among us, (and we beheld His glory, the glory as of the only begotten of the Father,) full of grace and truth." In Hebrews 1:1, 2 we read, "God, Who at sundry times and in divers manners, (many ways) spake in time past unto the fathers by the prophets, hath in these last days spoken unto us by His Son, Whom He hath appointed heir of all things, by Whom also He made the worlds (ages)."

Since God has given the Scriptures to His people, those who preach and teach them have a special responsibility to God for that which they deliver. God has entrusted His revelation to them, and therefore they must be extremely careful how they use it. They must make the revelation known in a manner that is faithful to its meaning and at the same time beneficial to the hearers. I Corinthians 4:1, 2 declares, "Let a man so account of us (consider us), as of the ministers (servants) of Christ, and stewards of the mysteries (hidden truths) of God. Moreover it is required in stewards, that a man be found faithful." Then in II Timothy 2:15 we read these words, "Study (be diligent) to show (present) thyself approved unto God, a workman that needeth not to be ashamed, rightly dividing the Word of truth."

Preachers and teachers, though they announce a message that is not their own, must treat that message with inspiring awe and respect as if it were their own. The message must become, as it were, a part of the messenger before it can be given to others. Jeremiah said, "For since I spake, I cried out, I cried violence and spoil (plunder); because the Word of the Lord was made a reproach unto me, and a derision, daily. Then said I, I will not make mention of Him, nor speak any more in His name. But His Word was in my heart as a burning fire shut up in my bones, and I was weary with forbearing (holding back), and I could not stay (endure it)," (20: 9).

In Revelation 10: 8-11 we find these important words, "And the voice which I heard from heaven spake unto me again, and said, Go and take the little book which is open in the hand of the angel which standeth upon the sea and upon the earth. And I went unto the angel, and said unto him, Give me the little book. And he said unto me, Take it, and eat it up; and it shall make thy belly bitter, but it shall be in thy mouth sweet as honey. And I took the book out of the angel's hand, and ate it up; and it was in my mouth sweet as honey: and as soon as I had eaten it my belly was bitter. And he said unto me, Thou must prophesy again before many peoples, and nations, and tongues, and kings." Preachers are doing more than merely passing on someone else's message; they are instructing the hearers. Note the words of the Apostle Paul in Acts 20:20, "And how I kept back nothing that was profitable unto you, but have showed you, and have taught you publicly, and from house to house." It seems then that preachers of the gospel are virtually imparting life to those who hear and obey the gospel message. But the only authority in their instruction is that of the Word they preach. "For I have not shunned to declare unto you all the counsel of God." Thus, the spiritual authority of the message that changes lives comes from God, not from the preacher.

If a person is dependent on God for the benefits his preaching brings to others, he will express his dependence through constant prayer. He will also live righteously, so that his life is consistent with his message. I Thessalonians 1:5 states, "For our gospel came not unto you in word only, but also in power, and in the Holy Ghost, and in much assurance; as ye know what manner of men we were among you for your sake." I Timothy 4: 16 declares, "Take heed unto thyself, and unto the doctrine; continue in them: for in doing this thou shalt both save thyself, and them that hear thee." Yet, he must put thought and effort into his ministry and must work constantly at improving the quality of his performance.

A preacher faces many varied dangers as he endeavors to fulfill the ministry responsibility placed upon him by the Holy Spirit. Among them is the temptation to adjust his message to win the approval of the audience. This is the fault for which false prophets were consistently condemned in the Old Testament. By contrast, the true messenger of God says what needs to be said, whether or not it is what the people want to hear. Whatever Scripture he is expounding, he interprets and applies it honestly. He does not twist it to make it something different from what the Biblical author intended. At all times his concern is to gain God's approval, not to win people's praise.

When one answers the call of the Holy Spirit to

proclaim the gospel of Christ he is saying, 'YES, I WILL **RISE TO THE CHALLENGE.'** In other words, he is willing to stand in the gap for lost souls so that by all means he may win some to Christ. Satan does everything that he can to tear down and destroy such a person. John 10:10, "The thief comes to kill, steal, and destroy; but I (Jesus) have come that you might have life, and have it more abundantly." As the preacher relies upon the Spirit for strength and direction he is enabled with a special anointing to overcome all obstacles that are thrown at him. To preach the gospel is a tremendous challenge, knowing that every word spoken brings either life or death to the hearers.

When one **RISES TO THE CHALLENGE** he must remember that he is not just another person anymore. He has a special obligation to live what he preaches for his life is no longer his own. He is the servant of the people, and of the Lord. His life is an open book, read and known of all men. His every move is scrutinized and he is accountable to those to whom he ministers. What is even more important is that, he must remember that he is accountable to God, not only for his own life, but also for the lives of the flock to whom he preaches. **What an awesome responsibility!!**

Nonetheless, this responsibility is not to be shirked or feared, for the Lord will see the preacher through and will anoint him for the task to which he has been called. God will never ask one to do what he cannot do or go where he cannot go. He will not take us where His grace cannot keep us. Jesus said, "I am with you, I will not leave you nor forsake you," (Hebrews 13: 5). To preach the gospel is a tremendous challenge, but when we **RISE TO**

31

MEET THE CHALLENGE, we enjoy seeing souls saved, believers filled with the Holy Spirit and sick bodies healed because God confirms "His Word with signs following," (Mark 16). Praise the Lord!

P. T. Forsyth said, "Preaching is the gospel prolonging and declaring itself....it is an eternal, perennial act of God in Christ, repeating itself within each declaration of it," *(Positive preaching and the modern mind, New York: Eaton & Mains, p5f)*. It is only when the living God, Who Himself spoke in the history recorded in the Bible, speaks again through the preaching of the Bible, that a sermon becomes a sermon. Otherwise, it is a speech or an address on a religious topic; the speech of a man about God, not God speaking of Himself to man.

Baker's Dictionary of Practical Theology states, "Properly to preach the gospel means to view the Bible as a whole and to allow it to determine the central emphasis around which Christian preaching should center. In light of the Old Testament story focusing upon the exodus and coming Messianic deliverance and the New Testament centering in the New Covenant established by God's redemptive act in the death and resurrection of Jesus Christ, Christian preaching should center in God's redeeming action set forth in both Testaments, climaxed in Jesus' cross and resurrection."

True preaching searches for the eternal values in the Scriptures in order to relate them helpfully to life. Though the emphasis of preaching may shift, yet, it must stay within limits that are unalterably fixed. Three of which are: 1) That which the minister proclaims must be truly the Word of God; 2) The message must be complete. A half-message is like a half-truth, and may be as hurtful as an untruth; 3) The message must be rightly motivated. It doesn't matter how right or correct a message is, if it is delivered with wrong motives it will not be as effective in the changing of lives.

When one **RISES TO THE CHALLENGE** of **preaching** he will also use imagination in preaching. I said "IMAGINATION, not EXAGGERATION!" W. M. Dixon in his lectures on **'The Human Situation'** said, "The mind of man is more like a picture gallery than a debating chamber." To be a great preacher one must be able to use the gift of pictorial imagination, without being too wordy which takes away from the forcefulness of the message presented. Also, the use of illustrations and poetry make a message come alive as long as it is not a compilation of pious poems and moralizing anecdotes. The use of such is good, but overuse causes the message to be lost in a hodgepodge of illustrations that lulls the congregation to sleep. That is not the purpose of preaching. The purpose of preaching is to bring lost souls to Christ, to see lives changed by the power of God.

There was a preacher who once told me that he "did not believe in preaching doctrine." I countered with, "If we do not preach doctrine, we do not preach the Word of God." Why? To preach salvation is to preach doctrine. Other subjects such as, grace, the Cross, redemption, the Holy Spirit and divine healing, are all doctrinal. We must preach the entirety of the Word of God. Again, Acts 20:20 and 27 state, "And how I kept back nothing that was helpful to you, but declared it to you, and taught you publicly and from house to house, for I have not shunned to declare to you all the counsel of God," (NKJV).

RISE TO THE CHALLENGE and preach the whole counsel of God without fear or favor. Nothing else will suffice to keep the believer pure in heart, encouraged in spirit, and "looking for the blessed hope and glorious appearing of our great God and Savior, Jesus Christ," (Titus 2:13). Nothing else will change the lives of men and women and bring them into a proper relationship with the Lord Jesus Christ. Nothing else will put marriages back together, causing husbands and wives to love each other the way God meant them to. Nothing else will bring total healing to the total person, to the body, to the mind, and to the spirit. Therefore, **RISE UP** and preach the Word for all it's worth and watch the Lord confirm His Word with signs and wonders. **Preach as a dying man to dying men.** God declared through the prophet Malachi "For I am the Lord, I cannot change….," (3:6). In the New Testament book of Hebrews 13:8 we find these words, "Jesus Christ, the same yesterday, today, and forever."

CHAPTER FOUR
THE CHALLENGE OF PRAYER

WHAT IS PRAYER? The Twentieth Century Bible Dictionary says it is, "Humble and earnest communion with God for the purpose of seeking some blessing, for confession of sin, or for acknowledging mercies received." This dictionary goes on to say that though "prayers are made from various bodily positions such as kneeling, lying with the face downward, standing, and raising one's hands, the effectiveness of prayer is determined only by the gracious will of God and by a person's sincerity and faith, his spirit of devotion to God, his sense of repentance and his willingness to submit to God's will."

Acts 9:40, "But Peter put them all out, and knelt down, and prayed....," (NKJV)

Matthew 26:39, "And He went a little farther, and fell on His face, and prayed,....," (NKJV).

Matthew 6:5, "And when you pray, you shall not be like the hypocrites. For they love to pray standing in the synagogues and on the corners of the streets, that they may be seen of men...," (NKJV).

Psalm 28:2, "Hear the voice of my supplications, when I cry unto thee, when I lift up my hands toward thy holy oracle," (NKJV).

James 4:7, "Therefore submit to God. Resist the devil and he will flee from you," (NKJV).

World's Bible Dictionary states, "Prayer is that activity of believers whereby they communicate with God, worshipping Him, praising Him, thanking Him, confessing to Him and making requests of Him."

People may engage in prayer anywhere and at any time. Note several verses of Scripture in this regard. Genesis 24:12, 13a, "And he said (Abraham's servant) O Lord God of my master Abraham, I pray thee, send me good speed this day, and show kindness unto my master Abraham. Behold, I stand here by the well of water;....," Nehemiah 2:4, "And it came to pass, when I heard these words, that I sat down and wept, and mourned certain days, and fasted, and prayed before the God of heaven........," Luke 5:16, "And He withdrew Himself into the wilderness and prayed." Luke 18:1, "And He spake a parable unto them to this end, that men ought always to pray, and not to faint (grow weary)." In addition to developing the habit of speaking to God freely regardless of time or place, believers should set aside a time and place when they can be alone with God and pray. Here is where the CHALLENGE TO PRAY arises. Even Jesus recognized the need for set times of prayer. Matthew 14:23, "And when He had sent he multitudes away, He went up on a mountain by Himself to pray. And when evening had come, He was alone there." Mark 1:35, "And in the morning, having risen a long while before daylight, He went out and departed to a solitary place; and there He prayed," (NKJV). Daniel the prophet also recognized the importance of a special time and place of prayer. Note the words as recorded in chapter 6, verse 10, "Now when Daniel knew that the writing was signed, he went into his house; and his windows being opened in his chamber toward Jerusalem, he kneeled upon his knees three times a day, and prayed, and gave thanks before his God, as he did aforetime." We have already noted several Scriptures with reference to differing positions when praying. Other Scriptures are as follows: 1 Samuel 1:26, (standing); 1 Kings 8:54, (kneeling); 18:42, (prostrate with face between knees); Ezra 9:5, (fell upon knees); Luke 18:11, (standing with head up); 18:13, (standing with head bowed down); Ephesians 3:14, (I bow on my knees). Once again let me emphasize that the position of the body is not what matters, but the motive or position of the heart in the sight of God. The important thing is that we pray with a heart of gratitude.

Praying in faith does not mean that there is no need for persistence in prayer. On the contrary, faith involves perseverance. Believers do not have to beg from a God Who is unwilling to give. Nevertheless, they pray constantly, since their prayers are an expression of their unwavering faith. They know that their heavenly Father will supply His children's need.

Mark 14:38, "Watch and pray, lest you enter into temptation. The spirit truly is ready, but the flesh is weak," (NKJV).

Ephesians 6:18, "Praying always with all prayer and supplication in the Spirit, being watchful to this end with all perseverance and supplication for all the saints...," (NKJV).

Colossians 4:2, "Continue in prayer, being vigilant in it with thanksgiving," (NKJV).

I Thessalonians 1:2, "We give thanks to God always for you all, making mention of you in our prayers," (NKJV).

Philippians 4:19, "And my God shall supply all your need according to His riches in glory by Christ Jesus," (NKJV).

Other Scriptures which you may wish to look up for reference are: Luke 11:5-13; 18:1-8; and 1 Thessalonians 5:17.

In these days of materialism and vanity when everyone seems to be preoccupied with themselves and their own immediate concerns it is difficult to find anyone who is really prepared to spend time in prayer so as to combat the forces of darkness that rage all around us. We make statements such as, 'PRAYER CHANGES THINGS' and 'ALL THINGS ARE POSSIBLE TO THOSE WHO BELIEVE,' yet we are not willing to do battle and persevere in prayer until we receive victory in the area of our struggle.

Luke 18:1 tells us, "Men ought always to pray, and not to faint." Literally, we must "pray without ceasing" (I Thessalonians 5:17), and not grow weary in well doing lest the enemy come at our time of weakness and tempt us to give up altogether. If we really want the power of God upon our lives we are going to have to learn to spend time with the Lord in intimate fellowship with Him. That means P-R-A-Y-E-R.

Again, the Bible teaches, "The effectual fervent prayer of a righteous man (or woman) availeth much" (James 5:16). A section in the *Full Life Study Bible* entitled, 'EFFECTIVE PRAYING' sums up the importance of the dedication and consecration of believers in prayer. It starts with a quotation from I Kings 18:42b-45, "And Elijah went up to the top of Carmel; and he cast himself down upon the earth, and put his face between his knees, and said to his servant, 'Go up now, look toward the sea.' And he went up, and looked, and said, 'There is nothing.' And he (Elijah) said, 'Go again seven times.' And it came to pass at the seventh time, that he (the servant) said, 'Behold there ariseth a little cloud out of the sea, like a man's hand.' And he (Elijah) said, 'Go up, and say unto Ahab, Prepare thy chariot, and get thee down, that the rain stop thee not.' And it came to pass in the meanwhile, that the heaven was black with clouds and wind, and there was a great rain. And Ahab rode and went to Jezreel." Elijah knew his God and he knew how to pray. He did not pray only when there was a problem but he prayed and had intimate fellowship with his Lord when everything was going smoothly. Then when problems came he had the assurance that God would see him through. His prayer brought faith alive in his spirit so that he could trust the Lord for all of his need.

Prayer refers to the multifaceted communication of believers with the Lord God. In addition to such words as 'PRAYER' and 'PRAYING' this activity is described as calling upon God. Psalm 17:6, "I have called upon thee, for thou wilt hear me, O God:...." It is described as calling upon the name of the Lord. Genesis 4:26 says, "…. then began men to call upon the name of the Lord." In Psalm 3:4 it is called crying unto the Lord, "I cried unto the Lord with my voice, and he heard me out of his holy hill." Prayer is called lifting up one's soul unto the Lord. Psalm 25:1, "Unto thee, O Lord, do I lift up my soul." In Isaiah 55:6 it is called seeking the Lord, "Seek ye the Lord while

He may be found, call ye upon Him while He is near." Hebrews 4:16 calls it coming "boldly unto the throne of grace, that we may obtain mercy, and find grace to help in the time of need." Verse 22 of Hebrews chapter 10 calls prayer drawing near to God. Note the words of the verse, "Let us draw near with a true heart in full assurance of faith, having our hearts sprinkled from an evil con-science, and our bodies washed with pure water."

In answer to the question, 'WHY PRAY?' three particular answers are given: **First,** believers are commanded by God to pray. The command given by inspiration of the Holy Spirit comes from the lips of Psalmists. David said in 1 Chronicles 16:11, "Seek the Lord and His strength, seek His face continually." (Check also Psalm 105:4); Prophets, Amos 5:4, 6, "For thus saith the Lord unto the house of Israel, Seek ye me, and ye shall live: Seek the Lord, and ye shall live; lest He break out like fire in the house of Joseph..., " (cf. Isaiah 55:6); Apostles, I Thessalonians 5:17, "Pray without ceasing" (cf. Ephesians 6:17, 18; Colossians 4:2); and the Lord Jesus, Himself.

God desires our fellowship; by prayer we maintain our relationship with Him. Note the words of Jesus as given in Matthew 26:41, "Watch and pray, that ye enter not into temptation: the spirit indeed is willing, but the flesh is weak." In John 16:24, "Hitherto have ye asked nothing in my name: ask, and ye shall receive, that your joy may be full." (cf. Luke 18: 1).

Second, prayer is the necessary link to receiving God's blessings and power, and the fulfillment of His promises. **NOTE that Jesus promised His followers** that they would receive the Holy Spirit if they persisted in asking, seeking, and knocking at the door of their heavenly Father (Luke 11:5-13). After Jesus' ascension, we see that His followers continually devoted themselves to prayer in the Upper Room until with power the Holy Spirit was poured out upon them on the Day of Pentecost. Here is how the Bible puts it: "But ye shall receive power, after that the Holy Ghost is come upon you: and ye shall be witnesses unto me both in Jerusalem, and in all Judea, and in Samaria, and unto the uttermost part of the earth. These all continued with one accord in prayer and supplication, with the women, and Mary the mother of Jesus, and with his brethren. And when the Day of Pentecost was fully come, they were all with one accord in one place. And suddenly there came a sound from heaven as of a rushing mighty wind, and it filled all the house where they were sitting. And there appeared unto them cloven tongues like as of fire, and it sat upon each of them. And they were all filled with the Holy Ghost, and began to speak with other tongues, as the Spirit gave them utterance." When the Apostles gathered together after their arrest and release by the Jewish authorities they prayed earnestly for the Holy Spirit to give them boldness and influence when speaking the Word of God. Acts 4:31 says, "And when they had prayed, the place was shaken where they were assembled together; and they were all filled with the Holy Ghost, and they **spake** the Word of God **with boldness**." The Apostle Paul frequently requested prayers on his behalf, knowing that his work would not be successful unless Christians were praying for him. In James 5:14, 15, James states explicitly that physical healing can come in direct response to the **"prayer of faith."** James puts it this way, "Is any among you afflicted (suffering)? Let him pray. Is any merry (cheerful)? Let him sing psalms. Is any sick among you? Let him call for the elders of the church; and let them pray over him, anointing him with oil in the name of the Lord: and the prayer of faith shall save the sick, and the Lord shall raise him up;...."

Third, in His plan of salvation for humankind, God has ordained that believers be co-workers with Him in the redemptive process. In some respects God has limited Himself to the holy, believing, persevering prayers of His people. There are many things that will not be accomplished in God's kingdom without the intercessory prayers of believers. God desires to send forth workers into the gospel harvest; Christ teaches that this will only be accomplished to God's full purpose through the prayers of His people: "Pray ye therefore the Lord of the harvest, that He will send forth laborers into His harvest" (Matthew 9: 38). In other words, God's power to accomplish many of His purposes is released only through the **earnest and effectual prayers of His people** on behalf of the progress of His kingdom. If we fail to pray, we may actually be hindering the accomplishment of God's redemptive purpose, both for ourselves as individuals and for the Church as a body. Naturally, there are certain requirements that must be met for prayer to be effective. Without meeting these conditions our prayers will go unanswered. **First,** we must have a sincere, true, faith that God will answer when we call. In Mark 11:24 Jesus states, "What things soever ye desire, when ye pray, believe that ye receive them, and ye shall have them." To the father of a demon possessed boy, Jesus said, "All things are possible to him that believeth" (keeps on believing, without fear or doubt) Mark 9:23. The author of the Book of Hebrews teaches us to draw near to God "with a true heart in full assurance of faith" (Hebrews 10:22), and James encourages us to "ask of God, in faith, nothing wavering" (James 1:6; 5:15).

Second, prayer must also be made in the name of Jesus. Jesus, Himself, expressed this principle when He said, "And whatsoever ye shall ask **in my name,** that will I do, that the Father may be glorified in the Son. If ye ask anything in my name, I will do it," (John 14:13, 14). Our prayer must be made in harmony with the character, person, and will of our Lord. **NOTE,** Jesus did not say to pray to Him or to the Holy Spirit. HE SAID TO PRAY TO THE FATHER IN HIS NAME. Our heart becomes the prayer room and the Holy Spirit takes our prayers, (groanings which cannot be uttered), and presents them to the Father, Who answers them because they have been prayed in the name of His Son, our Savior, Jesus Christ.

Third, prayer can only be effective if it is made according to the perfect will of God: "And this is the confidence that we have in Him, that, if we ask anything according to His will, He heareth us," (1 John 5:14). **Note one of the petitions in Jesus' model prayer, "The Lord's Prayer," confirms this:** "Thy will be done in earth, as it is in heaven," (Matthew 6:10). **NOTE ALSO,** Jesus' own prayer in the Garden of Gethsemane as found in Matthew 26:42, "Not my will, but Thine be done." In many instances we know God's will because He has revealed it to us in the Scriptures. We can be sure that any prayer which is truly based upon the promises of God, in His Word, will surely be effective. Elijah was certain that the Lord God of Israel would answer his prayer with fire and later with rain because the prophetic Word of the Lord had come to him, and he was fully confident that none of the heathen gods was greater than or even as great and powerful as the Lord God of Israel. First Kings 18:1, 21-24 states, "And it came to pass after many days, that the Word of the Lord came to Elijah in the third year, saying, Go, show thyself (present yourself) unto Ahab; and I will send rain upon the earth. And Elijah came unto all the people, and said, How long halt ye (will you falter) between two opinions? If the Lord be God, follow Him: but if Baal, then follow him. And the people answered him not a word. Then said Elijah unto the people, I, even I only, remain a prophet of the Lord; but Baal's prophets are four hundred and fifty men. Let them therefore give us two bullocks; and let them choose one bullock for themselves, and cut it in pieces, and lay it on wood, and put no fire under: and I will dress the other bullock, and lay it on wood, and put no fire under: And call ye on the name of your gods, and I will call on the name of the LORD: and the God that answereth by fire, let Him be God. And all the people answered and said, It is well spoken (the word is good)." Verses 37, 38 continues the story, "Hear me, O LORD, hear me, that this people may know that thou art the Lord God, and that thou hast turned their heart back again. **Then the fire** of the Lord **fell** and consumed the burnt sacrifice, and the wood, and the stones, and the dust, and licked up the water that was in the trench." There are other times that God's will only becomes clear to us as we earnestly seek to determine what it is. Then, once we know His will about any given issue or situation, we can pray with confidence and faith that God will answer. From the verses of Scripture quoted above we see that when Elijah knew the will of God he spoke with confidence, (calm assurance), knowing that God would perform the necessary deed which would cause the people to again turn their hearts to Him in worship and adoration.

Fourth, not only must we pray according to God's will and in the name of Jesus, but we must be in the will of the Lord if our prayers are to be effective. God will give us the things we ask for only if we "seek first His kingdom and His righteousness," (Matthew 6:33). The Apostle John states, "And whatsoever we ask, we receive of Him, because we keep His commandments, and do those things which are pleasing in His sight," (1 John 3:22). Obeying God's commandments, loving Him, and pleasing Him are indispensable conditions for receiving answers to prayer. When James wrote that "the prayers of the righteous are effective," he meant both a person who has been made righteous by faith in Christ and one who is living a righteous, God-fearing, and obedient life, such as the prophet Elijah. In the Old Testament this same point was stressed. God made clear that Moses' prayers on behalf of the Israelites were effective because of his obedient relationship with the Lord and his loyalty to Him. Exodus 33:17 says, "And the Lord said unto Moses, I will do this thing also that thou hast spoken: for thou hast found grace in my sight, and I know thee by name." Conversely, the Psalmist said that "if we cherish (hold) sin in our heart, the Lord will not hear us," (Psalm 66:18). This was the attitude that caused the Lord to turn His ear away from the prayers of the idolatrous and wicked Israelites. **Note the words of the prophet** Isaiah

1:15, "And when ye spread forth your hands (pray), I will hide mine eyes from you: yea, when ye make many prayers, I will not hear: your hands are full of blood."

However, if God's people would repent of their sins and "turn from their wicked way the Lord promises to again turn His ear toward them, and heal their land," (11 Chronicles 7:14; Luke 18:14). NOTE that the prayer of the high priest for the forgiveness of the sins of the Israelites on the DAY OF ATONEMENT would not be heard until his own sinful condition had been cleansed.

Fifth, for prayer to be effective we must be persistent. This is the main point of the parable of the persistent widow in Luke 18:1-7. Let's read it together, "And He spake a parable unto them to this end, that men ought always to pray, and not to faint (grow weary); saying, There was in a city a judge, which feared not God, neither regarded (respected) man: And there was a widow in that city; and she came unto him, saying, Avenge me (vindicate me against) of mine adversary. And he would not for a while: but afterward he said within himself, Though I fear not God, nor regard man; yet because this widow troubleth me, I will avenge (vindicate) her, lest by her continually coming she weary me. And the Lord said, Hear what the unjust judge saith. And shall not God avenge (vindicate) His own elect, which cry unto Him day and night, though He bear long with them." Jesus' instruction to "ask… seek… knock." in Matthew 7:7 and 8 instructs perseverance in prayer. The idea is to ask and keep on asking, seek and keep on seeking, knock and keep on knocking. In other words, **don't give up.** The Apostle Paul exhorts us in Colossians 4:2 and First Thessalonians 5:17 to be steadfast in prayer. Note the words of the verses respectively, "Continue in prayer, and watch in the same with thanksgiving. Pray without ceasing." Likewise, the Old Testament saints recognized this principle. **Note**, that as long as Moses persevered in prayer with his hands lifted toward God, the Israelites were successful in their battle against the Amalekites. Exodus 17:11 "And it came to pass, when Moses held up his hand, that Israel prevailed: and when he let down his hand, Amalek prevailed." After Elijah received the prophetic word that rain was coming, he still persisted in prayer until the rain came. First Kings 18:41-45, "And Elijah said unto Ahab, Get thee up, eat and drink; for there is a sound of abundance of rain. So Ahab went up to eat and to drink. And Elijah went up to the top of Carmel; and he cast himself down upon the earth, and put his face between his knees, and said to his servant, Go up now, look toward the sea. And he went up, and looked, and said, There is nothing. And he said, Go again seven times. And it came to pass at the seventh time, that he said, Behold, there ariseth a little cloud out of the sea, like a man's hand. And he said, Go up, say unto Ahab, Prepare thy chariot, and get thee down, that the rain stop thee not…And the hand of the Lord was on Elijah." On another occasion as recorded in First Kings 17:17-23 this same great prophet of God persistently and earnestly prayed for God to give life back to the dead child of the widow of Zarephath until the Lord answered his prayer. We wonder, at times, why God does not seem to answer our prayers. Is it a possibility that we neglect to be persistent or that we have not prayed according to the will of the Lord but according to our own selfish desires? James said, "Ye ask, and receive not, because ye ask amiss, that ye may consume it upon your own lusts (pleasures)."

There are five elements that constitute effective prayer. **One,** to pray effectively we must praise and adore the Lord. Psalm 150 is a complete Psalm of praise to the Lord. Acts 2: 47, "Praising God, and having favor with all the people. And the Lord added to the church daily such as should be saved." Romans 15:11, "And again, Praise the Lord, all ye Gentiles; and laud Him all ye people." **Second,** closely related and equally important to praise and adoration is **thanksgiving** to God. Thank Him for what He has done (past blessings), for what He is doing (present blessings), and for what He is going to do (future blessings). Psalm 100:4, "Enter into His gates with thanksgiving and into His courts with praise: be thankful unto Him, and bless His name." (cf. Matthew 11:25, 26; Philippians 4:6). **Third,** sincere confession of known sins as well as our faults and failure is essential to the prayer of faith. Luke 18:13, "And the publican (sinner), standing afar off, would not lift up so much as his eyes unto heaven, but smote upon his breast, saying, God be merciful to me a sinner. 14) I tell you, this man went down to his house justified (declared righteous, just as if he never sinned)…" 1 John 1:8, 9, "If we say that we have no sin, we deceive ourselves, and the truth is not in us. If we confess our sin, He is faithful and just to forgive us our sins, and to cleanse us from all unrighteousness." (cf. James 5:15, 16; Psalm 51). **Fourth,** God also instructs us to petition Him according to our need, as James writes, "We do not receive the things we want because we do not ask, or we ask with the wrong motives," James 4:2, 3. (cf. Psalm 27:7-12; Matthew 7:7-11). **Fifth,** we must pray fervently for others. In other words, we must intercede on their behalf whether they are friend or foe. Luke 22: 31, 32, "And the Lord said, Simon, Simon, behold, Satan hath desired to have you, that he may sift you as wheat: but I have prayed for you, that your faith fail not: and when you art converted (saved, born again), strengthen your brethren." Luke 23: 34, "Then said Jesus, Father, forgive them; for they know not what they do. And they parted His raiment (clothing, robe), and cast lots." (cf. Numbers 14:13-19; Psalm 122:6-9).

IN WHAT WAY SHOULD WE PRAY? **Note** that the first thing that the Lord emphasizes is sincerity of the heart because we will not be heard simply for our empty words. Matthew 6:7 says, "But when you pray, use not vain repetition, as the heathen do: for they think that they shall be heard for their much speaking." We can pray silently according to 1 Samuel 1:13 or we can pray out loud according to Nehemiah 9:4 and Ezekiel 11:13. Note the words of these verses respectively. "Now Hannah, she spake in her heart; only her lips moved, but her voice was not heard...."

"Then stood up upon the stairs, of the Levites, Jeshua .....and Chenani, and cried with a loud voice unto the Lord their God."

"...Then fell I down upon my face, and cried with a loud voice, and said, Ah Lord God! wilt thou make a full end of the remnant of Israel?" We can pray in our own words or we can use the words of Scripture in prayer. We can pray with the mind (understanding), or we can pray in (with) the spirit (in other tongues), 1 Corinthians 14:14-18. We can pray with groanings which cannot be uttered in human words knowing that the Spirit will bring those prayers (requests) to the Father. The Apostle Paul says in Romans 8:26, "Likewise the Spirit also helpeth our infirmities (weaknesses) for we know not what we should pray for as we ought: but the Spirit itself (Himself) maketh intercession for us with groanings which cannot be uttered." Another method of praying is by singing unto the Lord. Note just a few Scriptures in reference to this: Psalm 92:1, 2, "It is a good thing to give thanks unto the Lord, and to sing praises unto thy name, O Most High: to show forth (declare) thy loving kindness in the morning, and thy faithfulness every night." Ephesians 5:19, "Speaking to yourselves in psalms and hymns and spiritual songs, singing and making melody in your heart to the Lord." (cf. Colossians 3:16). At times earnest prayer will be accompanied by fasting according to the following Scriptures: Ezra 8:21, "Then I proclaimed a fast there, at the river of Ahava, that we might afflict (humble) ourselves before our God, to seek of Him a right way for us, and for our little ones, and for our substance." Daniel 9:3, 4, "And I set my face unto the Lord God, to seek by prayer and supplication, with fasting, and sackcloth, and ashes: and I prayed unto the Lord my God, and made my confession, and said, O Lord, the great and dreadful (awesome) God, keeping the covenant and mercy (loving-kindness) to them that love Him, and to them that keep His commandments." Acts 14:23, "And when they had ordained (appointed) them elders in every church, and had prayed with fasting, they commended them to the Lord, on Whom they had believed." (cf. Mark 9:29). **And we must always pray in faith**, for if we pray without faith we cannot please God (Hebrews 11:6), and if we do not please God how can we expect Him to answer our prayer?

WHAT POSTURE IS APPROPRIATE IN PRAYER? We have already mentioned the differing posture's for praying and have found that the posture is not what makes the prayer effective or non-effective. The attitude or motive of the heart is what makes the difference in the effectiveness of our prayer. If we KNEEL, that is a sign of submission; If we SIT, we sit for instruction; When we STAND, we wait to run at His command; If we LAY PROSTRATE, we rest in His bosom; If we LIFT UP OUR HANDS, that is a sign of complete surrender to His will and purpose.

The important thing to remember is that we must have faith that God will keep His promises, have a sincere heart and earnest expectations, and a right relationship with the brethren. TO **RISE TO THE CHALLENGE** OF EFFECTIVE PRAYER our motives must always be pure before the Lord.

FOR WHOM SHOULD BELIEVERS PRAY? In their concern for the world that the rule of God will be effective in people's lives, they are to pray that God will send forth laborers into the harvest field to reap the souls of men for the Lord (Matthew 9:37, 38), and that God will guide those servants to make their work fruitful. Acts 12:5, "Peter therefore was kept in prison: but prayer was made without ceasing of the church unto God for him." Romans 15:30, 31, "Now I beseech you, brethren, for the Lord Jesus Christ's sake, and for the love of the Spirit, that ye strive together with me in your prayers to God for me; that I may be delivered from them that do not believe in Judea and that my service which I have for Jerusalem may be accepted of the saints; that I may come unto you with joy by the will of God, and may with you be refreshed."

Believers are to pray for the physical well-being of each other. That is, that they and their fellow believers might know God and His purposes better, be strengthened by God's power, have unity among themselves, grow in love and grace, develop wisdom, exercise right judgment, endure hardship with joy, and bring glory to God by lives of fruitfulness and uprightness.

Believers are to pray for their friends (Job 42:10), as well as their enemies (Matthew 5:44), and ask for mercy on those who have sinned and brought disgrace on themselves and on God. I Samuel 12:23, "Moreover as for me, God forbid that I should sin against the Lord in ceasing to pray for you: but I will teach you the good and the right way:" Exodus 34:9, "And he (Moses) said, If now I have found grace in thy sight, O Lord, let my Lord, I pray thee, go among us; for it is a stiff-necked (stubborn) people; and pardon our iniquity and our sin, and take us for Thine inheritance." (cf. Exodus 32:11-13). They are also to pray for the leaders of the nations, so that God's will would be done on earth and people might live at peace with each other. First Timothy 2:1, 2, "I exhort therefore, that, first of all, supplications, prayers, intercessions, and giving of thanks, be made for all men, for kings and for all that are in authority (a prominent place); that we may lead a quiet and peaceable life in all godliness and honesty (reverence), for this is good and acceptable in the sight of God our Savior."

When believers go through times of temptation and spiritual battles they are to pray for themselves that God will give them guidance for wisdom, protection, and for the necessities of life. Matthew 6:11 and 13 state, "Give us this day our daily bread. And lead us not into temptation, but deliver us from evil (the evil one):…" (cf. Acts 1:24, 25; James 1:5-8; Nehemiah 4: 8, 9). By prayer God's children can overcome all anxiety and live in the victory that Christ has won for them.

IT IS INDEED A CHALLENGE TO SPEND TIME IN PRAYER, but the benefits of prayer far outweigh the discipline and dedication to prayer. It is only through spending this time alone, in communion with the Lord that we can truly enjoy getting to know Him. If we never talk with Him we will never know His heart toward us. He desires to show Himself strong on our behalf; He desires to fight our battles for us; He desires to bless us. Therefore let us desire to spend time in His presence, in prayer, worshiping His Majesty. **RISE TO THE CHALLENGE** OF PRAYER and let Him bless your life and ministry.

WHEN SHOULD BELIEVERS PRAY? The quick and simple answer to the question is, **'at all times.'** Luke 18:1 says, "Men ought always to pray…" First Thessalonians 5:17 says, "Pray without ceasing." There are, however, times when the CHALLENGE OF A DISCIPLINED PRAYER seems to be greater than at other times. In any case, the children of God ought always be in an attitude of prayer. When the pressures of life or stressful situations almost overwhelm us it is difficult to maintain that effective life of prayer. Yet, if we are to experience the hand of the Lord moving in those troubled areas we must maintain that sweet communion with Him. It is not enough to come running to the Lord when we are in trouble and needing help as at times is the case. We must continually be in that attitude of prayer, both in the bad times and in the good times. Then like the sweet Psalmist of Israel (David), we'll be able to say, "I have never seen the righteous forsaken or his seed begging bread" because the Lord will always be our provider (Philippians 4:19).

Larry Hess says, "Pressure has a way of depressing us. It causes us to feel out of control. Each one of us is facing the pressures of our life-style, our work, our world. The pressure is on! Sometimes there is little we can do to avoid the pressure we face. At other times we face pressures because we are driven to extreme feelings and behavior. We are driven by our needs, our emotions, and our undisciplined life-styles. At times we feel that we must achieve or that we must win or that we must be in control." He continues his discourse with, "Learning how to pray even when under extreme pressure is a vital part of living out our commitment to Christ." In fact, when I say we are to pray, I am saying that we are to do these FOUR things:

1) Praise the Lord and proclaim his greatness;

2) Remember and rejoice with thanksgiving because of who God is and because of what He has done;

3) Acknowledge our sins and ask His forgiveness; and,

4) Yield to God's guidance and faithfully obey His Word.

Christ said, "Without me ye can do nothing" (John 15:5). Since we can do nothing for God in ourselves, we must be willing to sacrifice the self-glory. We must be willing to give up our plans in order to obey God, for God works through people who offer themselves totally to Him. Praying under pressure requires us to be clear-minded and self-controlled so that we may overcome the problems and pressures that would control us.

Josh McDowell said, "Being able to remember who God is and who you are in His sight is important as you meet the traumas and stresses of life." How important it is to remember such words as you **RISE TO MEET THE CHALLENGE** OF A DISCIPLINED PRAYER LIFE.

Are you ready to meet that challenge for an effective ministry and witness to those who do not know Christ as their Savior and Lord? Determine today that you will be that person who will stand in the gap for those who are sick, widowed, orphaned, or lost without the Lord. MEET THAT CHALLENGE and you will be blessed of the Lord!

CHAPTER FIVE
THE CHALLENGE OF VISITATION

Visitation is not something that everyone can do effectively or enjoys doing because it entails much more than simply going to someone's home and spending an hour or two with them. In this chapter we will look at what visitation means, what are the ministering aspects of visitation, who should or can visit, and the persons to whom visitation is a need.

There are three GREEK words which can be translated **'visit'** or **'visiteth'** but for our purposes here we need look at only one of these words. That is: **"EPISKEPTOMAI,"** (English transliteration), which means primarily, to inspect and signifies: 1) to visit with help, of the act of God (Luke 1:68, 78; 7:16; Acts 15:14; Hebrews 2:6); 2) to visit the sick and afflicted (Matthew 25:36, 43; James 1:7); 3) to go and see, pay a visit to (Acts 7: 23; 15:36); 4) to look out certain men for a purpose (Acts 6:3). In the **Septuagint** it signifies **'to visit with punishment'** (Psalm 89:32; Jeremiah 9:25).

Visitation encompasses ministering to the sick and the afflicted, whether at home or at hospital, ministering to the elderly, to those seeking repentance, to those who are bereaved, as well as general visitation to members of the congregation.

In our day, VISITATION generally means a time to get together to chat, have lunch, or perhaps a little fellowship. The 'FUNK & WAGNALLS' dictionary gives several definitions of visitation, some of which are: 1) to go or come to a place to see a person from friendship, on business, etc.; 2) to make a visit; pay a call; 3) to go, or to come to, so as to make official inspection; 4) to inflict punishment upon or for. There are several others but I believe that these are sufficient for the subject at hand.

When we talk of ministerial visitation it is never meant as a time for the visitation or infliction of punishment. It is not meant as a time to gossip or 'GET THE NEWS.' Rather, it is a time when folk receive exhortation and encouragement to help them over the rough areas of life. In the case of a person who does not yet know the Lord, it is a time when Christian light must shine through the life so that the sinner may see the glory of the Lord and long for forgiveness and acceptance into the Kingdom of God.

When visiting the sick, the minister's visit should be brief, though he must never appear to be rushed. He should sit or stand in a relaxed manner, and in full sight of the patient, so that the patient may converse with him if he so desires. Comments, the Scripture reading, and prayer should only take a few minutes. If the patient is convalescing or is a shut-in, the minister may wish to stay a little longer. However, no visit should be lengthy.

Ministering to those who are ill gives the minister valuable opportunities to grow spiritually and affords him experiences which will make him more effective in the pulpit. Sick people need spiritual encouragement and no one can be nearly so effective with them as can the minister. Always remember that Jesus said, "those that are sick need a physician." The minister can be the physician to them in the place of the Lord on earth as he encourages and prays for their recovery.

It is a CHALLENGE TO VISIT sick folk, whether at home, in the hospital, or in a nursing home, but it is a visit that is usually highly appreciated. The minister, as well as all believers, ought always to be ready and willing to be called upon to visit those who are sick and afflicted. Note again the words of Jesus in Matthew 9:12, "Those that are whole need not a physician, but those that are sick." Sick folk need someone who will be a source of encouragement, strength, and joy to them, so let us **RISE TO THE CHALLENGE** OF VISITATION and do everything that we can to help alleviate the pain and suffering of those with infirmities.

Let me emphasize at this point that visitation is not only for the sick. It must also encompass those who are in prison. In churches where I have pastored, I have encouraged the saints to go to the prisons and visit those who are incarcerated. Some of the inmates never have anyone come to see them. They feel that because they have committed a crime and have gone to prison they have been abandoned or forgotten. No one seems to care about them. As believers, we must show the love of Christ to them. We must show them that we care, we love them, and that the Lord Jesus loves and cares for them. We should remember that, that prisoner could be us but for the grace of God.

It is not enough to go to the prison and just sing or preach. We must be willing to meet with the inmates on a one to one basis so that we can begin to understand what happened for that person to be where he is. There is always a reason and if we do not understand the prisoner's situation, or problems, and what caused them to commit a crime, we will not understand how to effectively minister to them.

We must never meet prisoners with a condemning spirit or 'holier than thou' attitude. Most of them are already under enough guilt and condemnation. What they need is someone to show forth the love of God to them, and to encourage them to surrender their life to the Lord, for He alone can set them free (even while they are in prison). Romans 5:8 says, "But God commendeth (demonstrates His own) love toward us, in that, while we were yet sinners, Christ died for us." When they are visited they need a friend more than a preacher. Therefore, THE CHALLENGE IS TO BE A FRIEND, and let your life be the preacher. Win their confidence first, then share your testimony without preaching religion. In this way they may possibly be won to the Lord Jesus Christ.

Prison ministry is difficult for most people because they do not see through the eyes of the Lord. Any time that we see with the natural sight only, we are not seeing, nor can we see with the spiritual sight. To be effective in prison ministry we must see beyond the outward appearance as did our Lord. Jesus said, "The works that I see my Father do, I do" and since God is the Father of those who believe, we need to see Him do the works and then we do what He does. Amen! If we are going to pray for someone to get well, we need to see them made whole in the Spirit realm first, then we call their deliverance or healing into existence. Faith calls into existence that which is not as though it were. Faith does not see impossibilities; it sees possibilities. Faith does not see what is; it sees what can be through the power of Christ. Faith does not see sick folk or prisoners; it sees them healed and set free by the power of the Spirit of God. The Lord said, "It's not by might, nor by power, but by **My Spirit** saith the Lord" (Zechariah 4:6).

It is a CHALLENGE TO VISIT OLD FOLK in nursing homes but it must be done. Some people say, "That's not my ministry," and it may be true that one is not called to that specific area of ministry. However, we must, as servants of the Lord, be willing to do everything that we possibly can to encourage those elderly people, realizing that one day we could be in that same place unless the Lord returns very soon.

Personally, I have difficulty in almost all areas of visitation. Yet, as a minister of the gospel of Jesus Christ, I accept my responsibility before God and visit everyone that I can. WHY? Because, but for the grace of God, that's me. At times, I need someone to talk with, so I call upon another pastor that I can trust, or my District Superintendent. Likewise, elderly people need someone to talk with them or just to listen to them as they relate stories of by-gone days. Therefore, we need to be ready at all times for such ministry. It is **NOT JUST A CHALLENGE, it is a blessing!**

Most of us cannot visit the different countries around the world and see first hand the devastation of war, famine, earthquakes, floods, etc. on mankind. We hear about it on the radio and see pictures of it on the television news, we read about it in the local papers, and think there is little, if anything, we can do in these situations. The truth of the matter is that we can do much more than we think. We may not be able to go, but we can send financial support to help feed, clothe, and give medical assistance to those in need.

We can also financially aid those who are giving of their time and talents to go in our place. More importantly, we can all pray that those who go to help those who are in need will not only help the physical being but will also show forth the love of Christ that the needy will come to an acceptance of Him as Lord and Savior of their lives. Jesus says of those who help the needy, "for I was hungry and you gave Me food; I was thirsty and you gave Me drink; I was a stranger and you took Me in; I was naked and you clothed Me; I was sick and you visited Me; I was in prison and you came to Me. Then the righteous will answer Him, saying, Lord, when did we see you hungry and feed You, or thirsty and give You drink? When did we see You a stranger and take You in, or naked and clothe You? Or when did we see You sick, or in prison, and come to see You? And the King will answer and say to them, Assuredly, I say to you, inasmuch as you have done it to one of the least of these My brethren, you have done it to Me" (Matthew 25:35-40).

The primary purpose of visitation is not to chat about the weather, but to encourage and strengthen the saints and to lead sinners to a saving knowledge of Jesus Christ. The salvation of a soul is the greatest miracle of them all. Praise the Lord!!

Pastor, Christian worker, be ready to give yourself to this vital ministry of visitation for this is true evangelism; **reaching and touching those in need.** The Bible says,

"Pure religion and undefiled before God and the Father is this, to visit the fatherless and widows in their affliction and to keep oneself unspotted from the world" (James 1:27). Micah 6:8 puts it this way, "He (God) hath showed thee, O man, what is good; and what doth the Lord require of thee, but to do justly, and to love mercy, and to walk humbly with thy God."

THE CHALLENGE OF VISITATION MUST BE MET, not only by ministers and leaders, but **by all who call themselves by the name of the Lord.** Every child of God is called upon to give witness concerning the grace of God in their life. How can it be done if we never visit anyone? Acts 1:8 states, "Ye shall receive power after that the Holy Spirit is come upon you, and **ye shall be witnesses unto Me...**" Hence, everywhere we go, our lives are to be witnesses to the transforming power of Christ. Every person that we talk with ought to be considered a visit whereby we show forth the love of God, so that person may be touched by the hand of the Lord and be encouraged to serve Him more earnestly and effectively.

Beloved, let your visitation be a blessing to others and you will also be blessed and strengthened in the Lord. **RISE TO THE CHALLENGE** OF VISITATION. Do not let it become a dreary, mundane duty. Rather, let it be an exercise in excitement because of the blessing you can bring to someone in need. As a result, you will truly be blessed! Truly, when you give a blessing, you receive a greater blessing!

CHAPTER SIX
THE CHALLENGE OF FAMILY MINISTRY

The family is the second institution that was ordained of God. It was ordained in the 'GARDEN OF EDEN' when God said, "Let us make man in our image, after our likeness;…So God created man in His own image, in the image of God created He him; male and female created He them. And God blessed them, and God said unto them, be fruitful, and multiply, and replenish the earth, and subdue it…." Genesis 1:26-28. QUESTION: Why would I say that the family is the second institution ordained of God, rather than the first? ANSWER: Simply because there could not be a family without first the marriage of the two first created beings—man and woman. It would have been a monstrosity if God had first created a family of babies (the family) and then created the parents. It is natural that the marriage take place first, then comes the family—although in our present society this has been somewhat challenged and reversed. God did not create Mary and Carrie, or Adam and Steve. He created man and woman—Adam and Eve. Therefore, **marriage is the first institution ordained by God.** When God had sanctioned the marriage of the two

He then told them to have a family. Note the words as found in Genesis 2:18, 21-24, "And the Lord God said, It is not good that the man should be alone; I will make him an help (helper comparable to him) meet for him. And the Lord God caused a deep sleep to fall upon Adam, and he slept: and He took one of his ribs, and closed up the flesh instead thereof; And the rib, which the Lord God had taken from man, made He a woman (lit. He built into a woman), and brought her unto the man. And Adam said, This is now bone of my bones, and flesh of my flesh: and she shall be called Woman, because she was taken out of man. Therefore, shall a man leave his father and mother, and shall cleave unto his wife: and they shall be one flesh."

So, then, the first thing that God did for man, to make him happy, was to give him a wife. Having given him a wife, God said, **'Have a family'** or multiply. Hence, man's first duty is to God; his second duty is to his wife; and, his third duty is to his family. That being the case, the fourth duty of one called to public ministry is to wait on the ministry to which he is called. Note the words of Romans 12:7-18 in reference to the duties or responsibilities toward society of one called to public ministry: "Or ministry, let us wait on our ministering; or he that teacheth, on teaching; Or he that exhorteth, on exhortation: he that giveth, let him do it with simplicity (liberality); he that ruleth, with diligence; he that showeth mercy, with cheerfulness. Let love be without dissimulation (hypocrisy). Abhor (hate) that which is evil. Cleave (cling) to that which is good. Be kindly affectioned (affectionate) one to another with brotherly love; in honor preferring (giving preference to) one another; Not slothful (lagging in diligence, lazy) in business; fervent in spirit; serving the Lord; Rejoicing in hope; patient (persevering) in tribulation; continuing (steadfast) instant in prayer; Distributing to the necessity (needs) of the saints; given to hospitality. Bless them which persecute you: bless, and curse not. Rejoice with them that do rejoice, and weep with them that weep. Be of the same mind one toward another. Mind not high things (set not your mind upon things that seem important in the world), but condescend (associate with the humble) to men of low estate. Be not wise in your own conceits (estimation). Recompense (repay) to no man evil for evil. Provide things honest (have regard for good things) in the sight of all men. If it be possible, as much as lieth (depends on you) in you, live peaceably with all men." Wow!! If only society would live according to that exhortation from the Apostle Paul, the world would be a much different place.

Men, at times, become so engrossed with ministry to the flock over which the Lord has made them overseers that they see nothing or no one else. Everyone close to them is pushed behind their back, as it were, and the church takes first priority over everyone and everything else. The church becomes their life. As a result, the children suffer, the wife (husband) suffers, and home life in general suffers because of the neglect. The Bible teaches that we are, **first, to take care of our own household.** If not, we are worse than an infidel (one who disbelieves in any religion, atheist). Also, if we cannot care for our own household, neither can we care for the household of faith. 1 Timothy 3:5 and 5:8 respectively state, "For if a man know not how to rule his own house, how shall he take care of the church of God? But if any provide not for his own, and especially for those of his own house (family), he hath denied the faith, and is worse than an infidel (unbeliever)." This is strong language and as ministers of the gospel we must be very careful in these areas. For taking care of one's house is not just the matter of making money and buying things for them. It is also being there to nurture, teach, and lead in the way that the family should go. We need to be careful lest we get our priorities in the wrong order. This is the cause of many separations and divorces within the body of Christ. The moment that we lose our perspective, in relation to our home life, Satan will have a trap set with which he is ready to snare us. He is extremely adept at setting traps for the children of God and especially for the ministers of the Gospel. The sadness of this is that we often do not recognize such and, as a result, fail in areas of life where we ought to overcome.

The family unit is the basis of society. John Donne made a profound statement when he said, "No man is an island." In the days that we now live the family is being redefined and attacked more than at any time since Sodom and Gomorrah. The world system has changed the meaning of marital bliss and family relationships to include same sex (homosexual and lesbian) couples into which no children can be born. Yet, these individuals fight for the right to adopt children and raise them in an atmosphere of ungodliness and debauchery. QUESTION: How can a child, raised in a homosexual or lesbian lifestyle know the love of both mother and father? ANSWER: The child cannot know and enjoy a real family life when raised in such horrific conditions. Satan has caused chaos in the family structure, and what is so frightening about the whole sordid mess is that many main-line denominations are accepting the homosexual status as a normal lifestyle so much so that they ordain them into gospel ministry. God did not take a rib from Adam and form another man! **He formed WOMAN for man to enjoy.** The Bible teaches that homosexuality is an abomination in the sight of God. Leviticus 18:22 and 24 show that it is self-defiling. Note the words: "Thou shalt not lie with mankind, as with womankind: it is abomination. Defile not yourselves in any of these things:..." In the New Testament the same teaching of homosexuality as being unnatural and contrary to sound doctrine is found in the following passages of Scripture. Note them: Romans 1:27, 31, "And likewise also the men, leaving the natural use of the woman, burned in their lusts one toward another; men with men working that which is unseemly (shameful), and receiving in themselves that recompense (fitting) of their error which was meet (due). Without understanding, covenant breakers, without natural affection, implacable (unforgiving), unmerciful: who knowing the judgment (righteous justice) of God, that they which commit such things are worthy of death...." 2 Timothy 3:3 teaches, "Without natural affection, trucebreakers (irreconcilable), false accusers (slanderers), incontinent (without self-control), despisers of those that are good." 1 Timothy 1:10, "For whoremongers (fornicators), for them that defile themselves with mankind (sodomites, homosexuals), for men-stealers (kidnappers), for liars, for perjured persons (perjurers), and if there be any other thing that is contrary to sound doctrine." To commit a homosexual act under the LAW OF MOSES (GOD) was such a serious offence that it warranted the death penalty. Leviticus 20:13, "If a man also lie with mankind, as he lieth with a woman, both of them hath committed an abomination: they shall surely be put to death; their blood shall be upon them." Although such practice has in these last days become more acceptable to society, it is nonetheless evil and wicked in the sight of God.

Homosexuality became widely practiced in Old Testament times. Judges 19:22 reads, "Now as they were making their hearts merry, behold, certain men of the city, men of belial (wicked men), beset the house round about, and spake unto the master (owner) of the house, the old man, saying, Bring forth the man that came into thine house that we may know (have sexual relations with) him." The HEBREW word here translated **'know'** literally means **"to have intercourse or sexual relations with."** This is the same word that is used in Genesis 4:1 in which it is recorded that "Adam **knew his wife**; and she conceived, and bare Cain...." It is also used in the same sense in Genesis 24: 16; 1 Samuel 1:19b; and Luke 1:34. Scripture indicates, that, as a sign of the end times, the homosexual way of life will become openly practiced and generally accepted by society as a whole. We are already seeing this take place before our very eyes. 2 Timothy 3:1-5 states, "This know also, that in the last days perilous times shall come. For men shall be **lovers of their own selves**, covetous, boasters, proud, blasphemers, disobedient to parents, unthankful, unholy, without natural affection (homosexuality, lesbianism, beastiality, etc.), false accusers, incontinent (no self-control), fierce, high-minded, lovers of pleasures more than lovers of

God, having a form of godliness, but denying the power thereof: from such turn away."

The above verses sum up the problem of our society and the reasons for the lawlessness that abounds in government, in the school system, on the streets, in business; yes, and even in religious denominations. Churches are filled with those who have little or no respect for authority, the church, the man of God, or God, Himself.

The breakdown and destruction of the family institution brings anarchy to society. When God created man and woman, He intended that there remain a mutual respect within His people for the distinction He had made between the sexes. Deuteronomy 22:5 says, "The woman shall not wear that which pertains unto a man, neither shall a man put on a woman's garment: for all that do so are an abomination unto the Lord thy God." Some well-meaning Christians have used the above verse of Scripture to maintain that women should not wear slacks. Thus, there have been divisions, controversy, and confusion over this particular verse. Let us try to clarify this verse a little to see the real intent of it. The word **"pertaineth unto"** (HEBREW—keli) in the original language is used elsewhere not only of clothes, but also of decorations or utensils used by the opposite sex. The intent of this law was to maintain the distinction between the sexes. Today, it would apply to any unisex clothing that would cloud the distinction between men and women. The New Testament recognizes such distinction (1 Corinthians 11:3). During the days of Moses, garments (HEBREW—simlah) worn by men and women were very similar (robes), so this command was designed to keep a woman from appearing as a man for the purposes of licentiousness (to deceive the man). The major difference between male and female robes was their decoration or ornamentation, and not their cut. The principle taught by this passage is that the proper distinction between man and woman in all cultures should be maintained. The passage does not teach against slacks *per se* (or hats, shoes, gloves, etc.—all worn by both sexes), but against men or women wearing any item specifically ornamented for the opposite sex (e.g. a man wearing female slacks, lipstick, etc.). The wearing of slacks by ladies today is not an attempt to deceive men, although some may be immodest and improper in certain situations. The final criteria are that women look like females, that they are modest (1 Timothy 2:9, 10), and that their outward appearance reflects their inner character (1 Peter 3:3)— *(Liberty Bible Commentary, Published by Thomas Nelson, Inc., Nashville, TN. Copyright 1982—Old-Time Gospel Hour).*

As ministers of the gospel, we are to care for our family first, making sure that nothing will cause such problems as to bring division. If any problem arises it should be dealt with immediately so that peace and harmony can be maintained within the family structure.

Someone once said that the family is the most difficult to minister or witness to. **This ought not to be the case.** We know our family, we know their struggles, we know their weaknesses, and we know their strengths and victories. We must remember that they know ours, also. The Bible teaches that our lives are "an epistle (an open book), known and read of all men" (2 Corinthians 3:2). In ministering to one's family, whether brother, sister, mother, father, son, or daughter, the mask comes off. They know us and the life we live; therefore, there can be no show or air of superiority. Because we are known of them, and by them, we should be able to sit and easily discuss the great things of the Lord, showing them that God wants to meet their every need, whether spiritual, physical, financial, or psychological.

We must let our family know that we care for them and about them. We must also let them know that God cares for them. The Word of God teaches, "Cast all your care upon Him, for He careth for you" (1Peter 5:7). In Galations 6.2 we are instructed to "Bear one another's burdens, and so fulfill the law of Christ."

I believe that unless we, as ministers, begin to minister to our family we will lose them and, should that happen, we will be held accountable to God for our actions, or, lack thereof, in this area. The reason that many pastor's children have gone bad is because dad has spent all of his time running around helping everyone else, while not taking a precious moment to instruct his own family in the ways of the Lord. **We need to keep our priorities in proper order.** Yes, we must minister to and win others to Christ, but if we cannot be effective with our own family, we have failed in our work for the Lord. What is the point of winning the world and losing our own children or family?

We see several examples in the Word of God where parent's weaknesses and sins caused problems that resulted in the family not serving the Lord. NOTE the words of 1 Samuel 3: 13, "For I have told him, (Eli), that I will judge his house forever for the iniquity which he knoweth; because his sons made themselves vile, and he

(Eli) restrained them not." Eli was the priest of God, serving in the temple. He had time for all his priestly duties to the tribe of Israel, yet, did not take time for his family. Even though God warned him about the tragic consequences of his inaction, he still failed in this all important matter of putting his family first and giving them proper training and correction in the things of the Lord. The end result was the disastrous death of his two sons who were killed in battle, the Ark of the Covenant being captured and taken by the Philistines, and the subsequent death of Eli when he heard the terrible news.

Another example is found in Luke 15:12, 13, which says, "And the younger of them said to this father, Father, give me the portion of goods that falleth to me. And he divided unto them his living. And not many days after the younger son gathered all together, and took his journey into a far country, and there wasted his living (substance) with riotous living." First, the son was claiming that which was not his. The birthright always belonged to the eldest son. Here, we see the younger son claiming that which belonged to his brother. Really, this young man was in rebellion to the normal flow of things. His father wanting to be a good daddy, lacked the tenacity to correct his son. Maybe he was afraid that he would lose him if he was too harsh. After all, you have to love them. What the father did not realize was that he had really lost his son before he ever gave him the money which he had requested. He lost his son when he refused to correct him for his arrogance and pride many years earlier in life. Now, he is simply reaping that which he had sown by sparing the rod—the child is spoiled and getting his own way. Daddy gave the young man what he wanted rather than what he needed and he made a complete mess out of his life. However, this story has a happier ending than the one before, in that the young man came to himself in the pigpen and made his way back home to complete forgiveness in the father's house. WHAT A DIFFERENCE LIFE WOULD HAVE BEEN FOR THE YOUNG MAN HAD DADDY RAISED HIM ACCORDING TO THE BOOK OF PROVERBS!!

We see what happens when children are permitted to do as they please and fathers don't take the time to show them the difference. Proverbs 29:15 says, "The rod and reproof give wisdom: but a child left to himself bringeth his mother to shame."

Let me give you just another couple of examples from the Word of God of children that went bad, but were raised in godly homes. 1 Samuel, Chapter 8, tells us that the people of Israel rejected Samuel's sons as leaders because they did not walk in the ways of their father. Note the words as found in verses 3 thru' 5, "And his (Samuel's) sons walked not in his ways, but turned aside after lucre (dishonest gain), and took bribes, and perverted judgment (justice). Then all the elders of Israel gathered themselves together, and came to Samuel unto Ramah, and said unto him, Behold, thou art old, and thy sons walk not in thy ways: make us a king to judge us like all nations."

The final example that I would like to mention is David, the king. Here is a man that sinned against God many times and repented of the sin. Here is a man that yearned after God and God's mercy so much that God called him a man after His own heart. This was the man who really brought Israel together, conquered the nations around him, expanded Israel's borders, and made Jerusalem the capital city from which he ruled the kingdom. Yet, he failed in raising his children properly. As king, he was a great ruler; as father, he was a miserable failure. Note the words of Scripture as found in First Kings 1:5, 6, "Then Adonijah (the fourth) son of Haggith (one of David's wives) exalted himself, saying, I will be king (I will reign): and he prepared himself chariots and horsemen, and fifty men to run before him and his **father had not displeased** (rebuked) him at any time in saying, Why hast thou done so? And he also was a very goodly (good looking) man; and his mother bare him after Absalom." The story is quite clear as found here. The young man wanted to take over his father's throne and his father did not even rebuke or correct him in this matter. You can also read how that Absalom, the third child born to this same woman tried to take the kingdom from his father and succeeded for a while. Rather than his father being the dad that he should have been, he ran away from his son and let him have the kingdom. Again, I repeat, David was a warrior for Israel but a dismal coward and failure when it came to ruling his own family. Maybe, as men of God, we could take a lesson from these examples in the Biblical record.

I personally know one father whose children have gone bad. The parents love the Lord. The father is a very godly person, a tremendous student of the Word of God. Yet, neither of the parents seem to understand the Scripture which says, "Foolishness is bound in the heart of a child but the rod of correction shall bring it out." All the father can say is, "You **have to love them,**" and while this is a true statement, the Bible also teaches that real "love corrects, and reproves with all longsuffering." Love does not let the child do as he pleases; love corrects the child when he/she goes wrong. Otherwise, the parents are accountable to God for not raising their children according to the principles and precepts of the Word of God which teaches, "Train up a child in the way he should go: and when he is old he will not depart from it" (Proverbs 22:6). Almost every time there is a prayer request taken and when visiting at the home of this particular couple about the only thing one hears is the children. They weep and cry now that the children are grown older about how bad they are and the things that they are into. It is time to begin to train them properly, when they are young so that when they are older, parents will not have to suffer such heartache.

Father's duties include much more than simply providing for their children. Note the words of the Apostle Paul in II Corinthians 12:14, "Behold the third time I am ready to come to you;....: for the children ought not to lay up for the parents, but the parents for the children." It also includes teaching the basic principles and precepts of God's Word and training them in the proper ethics of life. Deuteronomy 4:9; 6:7; and 31:13 respectively points out the principle above. Note the words, "Only take heed to thyself, and keep thy soul diligently, lest thou forget the things which thine eyes have seen, and lest they depart from thine heart all the days of thy life: but **teach** them **thy sons, and thy son's sons. And thou shalt teach them** diligently **unto thy children,** and shalt talk of them when thou sittest in thine house, and when thou walkest by the way, and when thou liest down, and when thou risest up. And that their children, which have not known any thing, may hear, and learn to fear the Lord your God, as long as ye live in the land whither ye go over Jordan to possess it." It includes nurturing, admonition, and instruction. Again we go to the Word of God for Scripture to back up this statement. Ephesians 6:4, "And ye fathers, provoke not your children to wrath (anger): but bring them up in the nurture (training) and admonition of the Lord." Colossians 3:21, "Fathers provoke not your children to anger, lest they be discouraged." Isaiah 28:9, "Whom shall he teach knowledge? And whom shall he make to understand doctrine (the message)? Them that are weaned from the milk and just drawn from the breasts. 10) For precept must be upon precept, precept upon precept, line upon line, line upon line; here a little, and there a little." It also includes love and control of the children—Titus 2:4, "That they may teach the young women to be sober, to love their husbands, to love their children...." 1 Timothy 3:4, "One that ruleth well his own house having his children in subjection with all gravity (reverence)." Pastors must also maintain a good, loving relationship with their spouse. Many times pastor's wives are neglected while the pastor ministers to the flock over which he is overseer. This can and often does lead to resentment, bitterness, misunderstanding, hatred for the ministry, and break-up of the home. It is not easy to put a broken egg back together, nor a broken home.

Indeed, God wants us to care for those whom He has put in our charge. THAT INCLUDES our spouse and children. If our family falls apart through our neglect, so also will the rest of our ministry. Therefore, let us be children of the Lord **first,** minister to our own family **second,** and then minister to the rest of the flock of God.

Joshua was leader of more than two million people. By all standards he was a successful pastor. The reason for his success is found in chapter 24, verse 15 where he took a stand for his family. To the Israelites, he said, "You decide for yourself what you want to do, but as for me and my house, we WILL serve the Lord."

In John 1:40, 41 we see Andrew leading his **brother, Peter** to Christ. Note the words, "One of the two which heard John speak, and followed him, was Andrew, Simon Peter's brother. He first findeth his own brother Simon, and saith unto him, We have found the Messiah, which is, being interpreted (translated), the Christ (lit. Anointed One)." Here we see the principle of first leading one's family to the Lord. After that we can lead the world to Christ.

The Philippian jailer and **his entire family** accepted Christ as Savior, and was baptized in water — Acts 16:25-33. Note the words of Scripture: "And at midnight Paul and Silas prayed, and sang praises unto God: and the prisoners heard them. And suddenly there was a great earthquake, so that the foundations of the prison were shaken: and immediately all the doors of the prison were opened, and everyone's bands were loosed. And the keeper of the prison awaking out of sleep, and seeing the prison doors open, he drew out his sword, and would have killed himself, supposing that the prisoners had been fled. But Paul cried with a loud voice, saying, Do thyself no harm: for we are all here. Then he called for a light, and sprang in, and came trembling, and fell down before Paul and Silas, and brought them out, and said, Sirs, what must I do to be saved? And they said, Believe on the Lord Jesus Christ, and thou shalt be saved, and thy house. And they spake unto him the Word of the Lord, and to all that were in his house. And he took them the same hour of the night, and washed their stripes; and was baptized, he and all his, straightway."

The **entire family** of the Nobleman accepted Christ in John 4:53. "So the father knew that it was at the same hour, in which Jesus said unto him, Thy son liveth: and himself believed, and his whole house."

The man out of whom Jesus had cast a legion of evil spirits (demons) was told to go home and **witness to his family** how great things the Lord had done for him. — Luke 8:39, "Return to thine own house, and show how great things God hath done unto thee. And he went his way, and published throughout the whole city how great things Jesus had done for him."

The above stories of the Philippian jailer, the nobleman, and the demoniac all speak of **HOUSEHOLD SALVATION.** If a pastor is to be really effective in his ministry, he has to take a stand against all the forces of darkness for his family. His ministry must start at Jerusalem (his home), and then spread to Judaea (surrounding communities), Samaria (the country), and the uttermost parts of the earth. Pastors, Christian workers, CLAIM your FAMILY FOR THE LORD. Become the person that will "stand in the gap and make up the hedge" that they may be saved. In many cases your ministry will be judged on the merits of your family. Pray for them, talk with them, and take them back from the clutches of Satan that they may serve the Lord. **RISE TO THE CHALLENGE!!** God did not call you to be in the Kingdom of God and your family to be left behind. **He is not willing that any should perish but that all should**

come to eternal life. John 3:14-17 states, "And as Moses lifted up the serpent in the wilderness, even so must the Son of man be lifted up: that whosoever believeth in Him should not perish, but have eternal life. For God so loved the world (people), that He gave His only begotten Son, that whosoever believeth in Him should not perish, but have everlasting life."

I repeat, **RISE TO THE CHALLENGE** of family ministry and win them to Christ. Do it now! Do it by faith! Call it done before you see it in the natural and expect a miracle. That's what faith does: It calls things that are not as though they were. It does not look at what is, but what can be. It does not see the impossibilities, it sees possibilities. Remember, Jesus never fails. He is "the same yesterday, today, and forever," (Hebrews 13:8). Jesus is coming! There will never be a better time than today to reach out to your loved ones and show them the love of Christ. Remember, He came to set them free from Satan's grip so that they might spend eternity with Him. RISE UP, take the challenge and see what the Lord will do. You may be amazed at the Lord using you to win your loved ones to Him.

CHAPTER SEVEN
THE CHALLENGE OF BIBLE STUDY

2 Timothy 2:15, "Study to show thyself approved unto God, a workman that needeth not to be ashamed, rightly dividing the Word of truth."

The GREEK word translated 'study' in the above verse means, "give diligence to" the Word of God. To do so will enable believers to remember the truth of Scripture so as to give an answer to those who are outside the household of faith, whenever called upon, without fear of failing or giving an incorrect interpretation of Scripture. The English transliteration of the GREEK word for 'rightly divide' is *orthotomeo* which means "to cut straight" or handling aright (the Word of truth); the meaning passed from the idea of cutting or dividing, to the more general sense of dealing with a thing. What is intended here is not dividing Scripture from Scripture, but teaching Scripture accurately. In other words, our text in 2 Timothy 2:15 teaches that believers are to **give diligence to teaching the Word of truth accurately.**

FUNK AND WAGNALLS dictionary defines the word 'study' as: 1) to apply the mind in acquiring a knowledge of; 2) to examine; 3) to look at attentively; 4) to endeavor to memorize; 5) to give thought and attention to; 6) to follow a regular cause or course of instruction; 7) to meditate.

In the case of studying the Scriptures, one is to give attention to, seek, or search and research for the true meaning of Scripture by comparing Scripture with Scripture, and letting Scripture interpret Scripture. Examine the Word of truth carefully so as to be sure that we do not make a private interpretation of the text, for the Bible teaches that the prophecy of Scripture is of "no private interpretation," (2 Peter 1:20). Again, one studying the Word of truth must remember that this is God's Word to man, NOT MAN'S WORD TO MAN, and that "all Scripture is given by inspiration of God, and is profitable for doctrine, for reproof, for correction, for instruction in righteousness; that the man of God may be perfect, thoroughly furnished unto all good works" (2 Timothy 3:16, 17).

Matthew Henry states, "The care of ministers must be to approve themselves unto God, to be accepted of Him, and to show that they are so approved unto Him. Therefore, there must be constant care and industry: 'Study to show thyself such an one, a workman that needs not be ashamed.' Workmen that are unskillful, or lazy, have need to be ashamed; but those who mind their business, and keep to their work, are workmen that need not be ashamed."

WHAT IS THE PURPOSE OF STUDY? To do such is a command, **but what is the purpose of such a command?** The last part of verse 15 above gives us a clear reason for diligent research of God's Word. **NOTE:** *It is to be able to rightly divide, or accurately, interpret the Word of truth.* To this, MATTHEW HENRY says, "Not to invent a new gospel, but to rightly divide the gospel that is committed to their trust. To speak terror to those to whom terror belongs, comfort to whom comfort; to give everyone his portion in due season, Matthew 24:45. NOTE: **First,** the Word which ministers preach is the WORD OF TRUTH, for the author of it is the GOD OF TRUTH. **Second,** it requires wisdom, study, and care, to divide the Word of truth rightly."

HOW DOES ONE STUDY TO GAIN A THOROUGH UNDERSTANDING OF GOD'S WORD? **First,** to properly study any course, one must have the right or correct tools. To study God's Word is no different. If one wishes to gain a thorough understanding of the Bible, certain tools are required which are of inestimable value. **Second,** one must be willing to spend time and energy in research as he/she seeks all information possible on a given subject such as: heaven, hell, salvation, Holy Spirit, healing, etc.

Let us look briefly at a few of the necessary tools for proper study of the Bible. Remember, that everyone has his own preference and that this is just a sampling of the many varied tools available.

Remember also, that it is not enough to say, "I read the Bible and that's enough for me." The Apostle Paul, by inspiration of the Spirit, stated that we are to *"study the Scriptures."*

One of the finest tools available and which should be in every believer's library, especially the ministerial student, is the Bible Commentary by MATTHEW HENRY. I realize that there are other fine commentaries available but I believe that since Mr. Henry's has stood the test of time for more than two hundred and fifty years and has been the most widely used of all Bible Commentaries, this in and of itself, speaks of the value placed upon it. Concerning this commentary, Charles H. Spurgeon stated, "every minister ought to read Matthew Henry entirely and carefully through once, at least."

Rev. Leslie F. Church says, "In spite of increasing knowledge, Matthew Henry commentary's profound insight into spiritual and eternal truth makes its essential teaching invaluable today. It is a practical and devotional work written by a man who has been described as one of the greatest commentators of all time. He, Matthew Henry, wrote with confidence and authority on the basic principles of conduct and belief, but with a modesty which commanded, and still should command, respect. He, Matthew Henry, once said, 'I have no sufficiency of my own, but by the grace of God I am what I am, and that grace will, I trust, be sufficient for me.' Matthew Henry described his work as methodized and practical expositions…in plain and homely dress. He stated that the purpose of his work was 'to promote knowledge of the Scriptures, in order to the reforming of men's hearts and lives.'

Mr. Henry was not dogmatic in his interpretation of problematic Scriptures, but rather agreed with Agustine that the Word of God had "enough in it that makes it easy to nourish the meanest to eternal life" and enough, also, to demand the industry and humility of the greatest scholars.

A second required tool for Biblical study is a good dictionary. Once again, there are many good dictionaries available. I will not place the same emphasis upon one over the other, as with the commentaries, for it is always a matter of preference among Bible students. Zondervan has a good pictorial Bible dictionary. Unger's is very good. So also is Smith's Bible dictionary an excellent tool for use in study.

My own preference is the Twentieth Century Bible dictionary which I use in conjunction with World's Bible dictionary. One cannot do justice to study without at least two other dictionaries which are: **First,** W. E. Vine's expository dictionary of Old and New Testament words. I could not properly prepare my messages without the use of this dictionary of Greek words with their meanings. **Second,** the companion to Vine's which is Wilson's Old Testament word studies is superb. By that, I mean that it is of tremendous value in both private and devotional study of God's Word.

A good concordance is needed for quick reference. Probably the best in the world is "Strong's Exhaustive Concordance." Every word of Scripture that could possibly be referenced in the Bible is listed in this concordance.

Other good books which aid the student of the Bible in understanding God's Word and which are vitally important are: *Bible Manners and Customs, People and Places of the Bible, and a book of word studies.* One must not only study a verse or story that is written, but also the **words of the verse or story**, so as to ascertain the meaning of the words. Then, as the verse or story is studied in its proper context the student will gain a greater understanding and appreciation for what the writer is saying. THIS INDEED IS A GREAT CHALLENGE!!

At this point, I would be quick to add that tools are

useless unless they are put to use. One may have a pickaxe and shovel but if they are not used a hole will never be dug. One may have a snow shovel but if it is not put to use the snow will not be removed. Likewise, one may have enough books to fill the world but if they sit on the shelf and are not used knowledge will not be gained.

If one wishes to go fishing, he will first buy all of the necessary equipment, then go fishing. He would be a fool to go fishing without his equipment and then complain that he did not catch any fish. Are you getting the message? I believe you are.

As is the one who goes fishing without his equipment, so also is the one who tries to witness to someone or preach the gospel without proper preparation. He will be a failure. A winner always prepares to win. Remember this, God uses those who are willing to prepare themselves for service in His Kingdom.

For a person to be adequately prepared to give witness to the grace of God in his life, or to proclaim the message of the gospel, so as to see results in the salvation of lost souls, healing the sick, etc. one must exert time and energy in preparation for the task. Not only must one be **willing** to study—**ONE MUST STUDY. This is a command of God!!** (2 Timothy 2:15).

I have heard people quote the Scripture which says, "Open your mouth, and I will fill it," (Psalm 81:10). They have made such statements as, "I don't need to study, I don't need to prepare a message because God said Open your mouth, and I will fill it." God did not mean this to be used as an excuse for laziness by those who don't want to spend time studying the Word to have substance to present to the people, otherwise He would not have given the command in 2

Timothy 2:15. God does not give contradictory commands. The above verse is for times when we are called before kings and rulers, and other unbelievers when we do not have opportunity to study before giving an answer. Then, we are told to not worry about what we shall say for the Lord will bring that which is needed to our remembrance and all we will have to do is "Open our mouth, and He will fill it." Laziness and ignorance won't cut it when we stand before a holy God to give an account for what we have done. I repeat, the above Scripture is not an excuse for one who will not spend time in the presence of the Lord studying His Word so as to know Him better and to understand what He is saying to the Church.

God cannot, and will not fill your mouth with that which is not in your heart. David said, "Thy Word have I hid in my heart, that I might not sin against Thee," (Psalm 119:11). God said that He would "bring all things to our remembrance," (John 14:26), and in this way we could "Open our mouth, and He will fill it." If we have not studied the Word and hid it in our heart, there is nothing there for the Lord to bring to our remembrance.

Now, let's put it all together, shall we, and see if we can gain an understanding of the message here related. Unless we study the Word to show ourselves approved unto God, as workmen that need not be ashamed, we are not hiding the Word of God in our heart. If we do not hide the Word of God in our heart, then we have nothing for the Lord to bring to our remembrance and if nothing comes to our remembrance, we will have no words in our mouth to speak. I might go a little farther and say that if we do speak words, they will be empty words without meaning or substance.

WHAT SHOULD WE DO THEN? **Again, preparation is the key.** When one has followed the direction of Scripture in preparation, then one is ready in any given situation to give an answer of the hope that lies within. In other words, that person **will never be caught off guard,** but will be "instant in season and out of season" (2 Timothy 4:2).

For those reading these words and saying that you cannot study or you do not know how to study, then for the sake of the sheep do not enter the ministry until you learn to be a good steward of God's Word. We cannot give to others that which we do not possess ourselves. No employer will hire someone who is not willing to train for the position applied for. Nor can God use a person who is unwilling to train for the ministry position to which he is called or desires to enter. THE CHALLENGE IS TO "PREPARE YOURSELF FOR THE TASK!!"

IT IS A CHALLENGE! It takes time and a lot of hard work to prepare oneself for ministry. At times, there is frustration and tears but when we learn to pray, "casting all our care upon Him," He comes to our rescue and helps us to overcome, as we prepare for the task of ministry that is ahead. Are you ready? THE CHALLENGE OF STUDY BECOMES A BLESSING WHEN YOU ARE PREPARED.

CHAPTER EIGHT
THE CHALLENGE OF TEACHING

Ephesians 4:11 says, "And He (God) gave some, apostles; and some, prophets; and some, evangelists; and some, pastors **and teachers."**

All pastors must be able to teach. This is a requirement of Scripture. Therefore, all pastors must be teachers or teaching pastors. God desires that His people learn about Him and His Word, and therefore He has given teachers to instruct them. Deuteronomy 33:10 says, "They shall teach Jacob Thy judgments, and Israel Thy law:." There are people of different types who have different ways or methods of teaching, but their teaching must have its origin in God Himself. For God alone is the TRUE TEACHER. **Note the words of Scripture:** "Show me Thy ways, O Lord; teach me Thy paths" (Psalm 25:4). "It is written in the prophets, **and they shall all be taught of God.** Every man therefore that hath heard, and hath learned of the Father, cometh unto me," John 6:45. (cf. 2 Timothy 3:16).

The Word of God reveals a variety of teachers. Even though God has given special teaching abilities to some, He does not expect that they be the only teachers. Parents are to be teachers and teach their children the way of

God. Deuteronomy 11:18, 19 states, "Therefore shall ye lay up these my words in your heart and in your soul, and bind them for a sign upon your hand, that they may be as frontlets between your eyes. **And ye** shall **teach them** your children, speaking of them when thou sittest in thine house, and when thou walkest by the way, when thou liest down, and when thou risest up." (cf. Ephesians 6:4). Any godly person may teach others the way of the Lord, though not necessarily in public meetings. Proverbs 10:21, "The lips of the righteous feed many:...." Acts 18:26, "And he (Apollos) began to speak boldly in the synagogue: whom when Aquila and Pricilla had heard, they took him unto them, and expounded (explained, taught) unto him the way of God more perfectly (accurately)." Colossians 3:16, "Let the Word of God dwell in you richly in all wisdom; **teaching and admonishing** one another in psalms and hymns and spiritual songs, singing with grace in your hearts to the Lord."

We find in the Old Testament era that Israel's religious and civil leaders had a wide ranging responsibility to teach the LAW OF GOD to the people. **Notice the following Scripture references:** Exodus 18:20, "And thou shalt teach them ordinances and laws, and shalt show them the way wherein they must walk,." Deuteronomy 33:10, "They shall teach Jacob thy judgments, and Israel thy law:." 2 Chronicles 17:7-9, "Also in the third year of his (Jehoshaphat's) reign he sent to his princes, even to Benhail, and to Obadiah, and to Zachariah, and to Nathanel, and to Michaiah, to **teach** in the cities of Judah. And with them he sent Levites,...And they **taught** in Judah and had the book of the law of the

Lord with them, and went about throughout all the cities of Judah, **and taught the people**...." Prophets taught in the name of God, bringing His message to a people who were constantly turning from the path of devotion to Him. Wisdom teachers gave instruction of a different kind, but it all helped to guide God's people in the way of righteousness and holiness. Proverbs 2:1, 2 says, "My son, if thou wilt receive my words, and hide (treasure) my commandments with thee; so that thou incline thine ear unto wisdom, and apply thine heart to understanding; 5) Then shalt thou understand the fear (reverential awe) of the Lord, and find the knowledge of God." 4:10, 11, "Hear, O my son, and receive my sayings; and the years of thy life shall be many. I have taught thee in the way of wisdom; I have led thee in right paths." Ecclesiastes 12:9, 13, "And moreover, because the preacher was wise, he still taught the people knowledge; yea, he gave good heed, and sought out, and set in order (arranged) many proverbs. Let us hear the conclusion of the whole matter: Fear God, and keep His commandments: for this is the whole duty of man." (cf. Proverbs 7:1-5).

Another group to gain prominence was the scribes, or teachers of the law. The earlier scribes were godly men who explained and applied God's law sensibly. Ezra 7:6, 10, "This Ezra went up from Babylon; and he was a ready (skilled) scribe in the Law of Moses, which the Lord God of Israel had given: and the king granted him all his request, according to the hand of the Lord his God upon him. For Ezra had prepared his heart to seek (study) the law of the Lord, and do it, and to teach in Israel statutes and judgments." Nehemiah 8:1-3, 8, "And all the people gathered themselves together as one man into the street (plaza) that was before the water gate; and they spake unto Ezra the scribe to bring the book of the law of Moses, which the Lord had commanded to Israel. And Ezra the priest brought the law before the congregation both of men and women, and all that could hear with understanding, upon the first day of the seventh month. And he read therein before the street (plaza) that was before the Watergate from the morning (lit. from the light) until midday, before the men and the women, and those that could understand; and the ears of all the people were attentive unto the book of the law." These were indeed godly men who were interested in knowing what the Lord wanted for His people, and in following the law of the Lord. However, by the time of Jesus, the scribes had developed into a class of traditionalists whose teachings prevented or hindered the people from entering the Kingdom of God. They stood at the door, as it were, not going into the Kingdom themselves, and not permitting the people to go in either. Note what Jesus said to them in Luke 11:52, "Woe unto you, lawyers (experts in law)! for ye have taken away the key of knowledge: entered not in yourselves, and them that were entering in ye hindered." (cf. Matthew 15:9; 23:1-7, 13).

The greatest teacher to ever live on planet earth was, and is, the LORD JESUS CHRIST. Although He enlightened people concerning the truth of the Scriptures, He also challenged them to make a response to His teaching. His teaching was a call to a life of discipleship. In Mark 8:34-38, Jesus teaches on the cost of that discipleship. Let us hear what He says, "And when He had called the people unto Him with His disciples also He said unto them, Whosoever will come after me, let him deny himself, and take up his cross, and follow me. For whosoever will save his life shall lose it; but whosoever shall lose his life for my sake and the gospel's, the same shall save it. For what shall it profit a man, if he shall gain the whole world, and lose his own soul? Or what shall a man give in exchange for his soul? Whosoever therefore shall be ashamed of me and of my words in this adulterous and sinful generation; of him also shall the Son of man be ashamed, when he cometh in the glory of his Father with the holy angels." (cf. Luke 9:57-62; 14:25-33). It is A CHALLENGE TO TEACH FOR LIFE-CHANGE, but all true teaching involves such a challenge.

Jesus, in training His disciples, CHALLENGED them to proclaim the good news, make disciples, and teach them the truth that Jesus, Himself, had taught. Matthew 28:19, 20, "Go ye therefore, and teach (make disciples of) all nations, baptizing them in the name of the Father, and of the Son, and of the Holy Ghost: teaching them to observe all things whatsoever I have commanded you: and, lo, I am with you always, even unto the end of the world."

Teaching in the church is for the purpose of building up the **'body of Christ'** through producing greater ability among believers to serve God and understand His Word. Ephesians 4:12 states, "For the perfecting (equipping) of the saints, for the work of the ministry, for the edifying (building up) of the body of Christ." Thus, we see that teaching is for **equipping the saints** until we all come in the unity of the faith (v.13).

In general, the instruction that teachers give should cover the whole spectrum of God's Word so that believers will develop the ability to discern between what is wholesome and what is not, and to **grow toward spiritual maturity.** In Acts 20:27 Paul said, "I have not shunned to declare unto you all the counsel of God." Matthew 28:20, "Teaching them to observe all things whatsoever I have commanded you…" Colossians 1:28, "Whom we preach (Jesus), warning every man, and teaching every man in all wisdom; that we may present every man perfect in Christ Jesus." Hebrews 5:12-14, "For by this time you ought to be teachers, ye have need that one teach you again which be the first principles of the oracles (sayings) of God; and are become such as have need of milk, and not of strong meat (solid food). For everyone that useth (continues to use) milk is unskillful in the Word of righteousness: for he is a babe. But strong meat (solid food) belongs to them that are of full age (mature), even those who by reason of use (practice) have their senses exercised to discern both good and evil." (cf. Ephesians 4:13, 14). Such instruction and development among believers will bring healthy growth to the church as a whole. Ephesians 4:15, 16, "But speaking the truth in love, may grow up into Him in all things, which is the Head, even Christ: from Whom the whole body fitly joined together and compacted (knit together) by that which every joint supplieth, according to the effectual (effective) working in the measure of every part (every part doing its share), maketh increase (causes growth) of the body unto the edifying of itself in love." Teachers ought never to waste time arguing over trivial matters, but concentrate on the type of teaching that produces the knowledge of God, a sincere faith, and a pure life. 1 Timothy 1:3-5, "…..that thou mightest charge some that they teach no other doctrine, neither give heed to fables and endless genealogies, which minister (cause disputes) questions, rather than godly edifying which is in faith: so do. Now the end purpose of the commandment is charity (love) out of a pure heart, and of a good conscience, and of unfeigned (sincere) faith." 4:6-8, "If thou put the brethren in remembrance of these things, thou shalt be a good minister of Jesus Christ, nourished up in the words of faith and of good doctrine, whereunto thou hast attained (carefully followed). But refuse (reject) profane and old wives fables, and exercise thyself unto godliness. For bodily exercise profiteth little; but godliness is profitable unto all things, having promise of the life that now is, and of that which is to come." 2 Timothy 2:23-25, "But foolish and unlearned (ignorant disputes) questions avoid, knowing that they do gender strifes (generate strife). And the servant of the Lord must not strive (quarrel); but be gentle unto all men, apt (able) to teach, patient, in meekness instructing (correcting) those that oppose themselves (are in opposition); if God peradventure will give them repentance to the acknowledging (so that they may know) of the truth;" 4:1, 2, "I charge thee therefore before God, and the Lord Jesus Christ, who shall judge the quick (living) and the dead at His appearing and His Kingdom; Preach the Word; be instant (ready) in season, out of season; reprove, rebuke, exhort with all longsuffering and doctrine."

A good teacher must be a good communicator. Richard Dresselhaus says, "As a draftsman must be skilled in the use of the tools of his trade, so the teacher must be skilled in the art of communication. If communication takes place, teaching has occured. Conversely, if there has been a breakdown in the process of communication, teaching has not occurred, no matter how intense the effort. GOOD TEACHING IS GOOD COMMUNICATION."

Richard A. Hatch defines communication as a process of "...a whole series of related actions which together serve the function of getting meanings shared among people." To illustrate this process, Mr. Hatch speaks of a communication model, or mental picture as outlined below:

A) Someone perceives an event...
B)....And reacts in a situation....
C)....To make available materials in
some form...
D)....Conveying content...
E)....Of some consequence....

A good teacher will put himself where the students are—and teach accordingly. One should never teach to satisfy himself but to provoke change in the living patterns of the students. Certain teachers have become experts at structuring the message, but they fail to develop facility in conveying that message meaningfully. An effective teacher is a strategist. He is anxious to experiment to find a better way—always searching for something new and stimulating.

The wise teacher will use a variety of teaching forms. He will experiment with new forms continually so as to spark interest and to help make the message meaningful. **The Word of God is the message!** And the CHALLENGE TO THE TEACHER is to get that message into the heart and mind of the hearer so that they will be CHALLENGED to live a life style pleasing to the Lord.

The wise teacher will also be aware of the abstract nature of many words that he uses, and because of their abstract nature, the variety of meanings attached to them. Therefore, the teacher will be careful to explain what he means by the use of such words so that only one meaning will be drawn from said words.

Every communication will be of some consequence. Effective communication occurs when the intended consequences of the communication situation has been attained. For example, when a teacher speaks correctively to a group of unruly children, the value of that communication rises or falls according to the response of the children. If their conduct becomes more acceptable, the teacher is happy to have gained the intended results. However, if their conduct remains as it was before the corrective words were spoken, that teacher will conclude that effective communication did not take place.

Richard Hatch suggests that there are three kinds of goals that lead to effective communication: **First,** to gain understanding—the learner must perceive; **Second,** to convince—the learner must deem that something is true and worthy of a change in his attitude; **Third,** to persuade—the learner will now want to act according to those newly formulated ideas. An adult may understand the plan of salvation; he may be convinced that his previous notions about salvation were wrong and that new attitudes must be formed; but it is not until he acts in faith and receives Christ as Savior that effective communication has taken place. Though there are distinct differences between teaching and preaching, there are also distinct similarities. Five ways in which there are similarities are as follows:

A) Both must be based solidly upon the Bible.

B) Both should have evangelism as its main goal.

C) Both require the anointing of the Holy Spirit to be truly effective.

D) Both require sound techniques of communication.

E) Both are most effective when the communicator is thoroughly dedicated to his task.

Please note that the two forms of communication: **preaching** and **teaching,** are different in at least two very important aspects. These are: **First,** teaching is not as limited to the spoken word as is preaching. That is, the teacher communicates by a wider range of methods than does the average preacher. For example, the teacher is much more likely to use visual aids, discussions, question and answer, or group projects than the preacher. The most obvious reason for this in most churches is that teaching generally takes place in a smaller group setting than the preaching does, and the preacher tends to be more limited to the spoken word (lecture) as a method. **Second,** teaching, as compared with preaching, uses a long term, continuative character. It does not concern itself with just one lesson, but with a whole progression of related lessons. Teaching takes the long view. It is concerned with a process; it repeats and interlocks its truths; it has a serial, scheduled quality.

While a preacher is primarily a **proclaimer** of the good news of the gospel, the teacher is the **explainer** of the news. WHAT AN AWESOME RESPONSIBILITY AND CHALLENGE FOR THE TEACHER!!

It is thrilling to know that the Christian teacher has a special relationship to the Lord Jesus Christ, Who was not only a preacher, but also the greatest teacher that ever lived. Note the words that Jesus quoted from Isaiah 61:1 in Luke 4:18, "The Spirit of the Lord is upon Me, because He hath anointed Me to preach the gospel (good news) to the poor; He hath sent Me to heal the brokenhearted, to preach deliverance to the captives, and recovering of sight to the blind, to set at liberty them that are bruised (oppressed, crushed), to preach the acceptable year of the Lord." John wrote of Nicodemus coming to Jesus by night and here is what he said to Him: "Rabbi, we know that Thou art a **teacher** come from God: for no man can do these miracles (signs) that Thou doest, except God be with him." These Scriptures point to the fact that He fulfilled the roll of both preacher and teacher. As teachers of God's Word, we share in what was His, the Lord's, most pronounced occupation, teaching. Like Him, we are teachers of truth, and we should be happy to share with Him in this special way.

A teacher also has a special relationship to the Christian Church. He helps to pass along, to perpetuate the values, attitudes, and activities which has made the Church of Jesus Christ a living, dynamic organism through the centuries. Despite its DIVINE ORIGIN, **without teachers the church would die.**

Whatever the age level one teaches, one should see himself as partly a preacher. That is, the teacher should proclaim, announce, stir, explain, and appeal to his hearers. The teacher must also have the long-view, looking beyond his own lifetime to the results of the character building that he is presently doing. The third thing concerning the teacher's viewpoint is that he must see his influence as concentrated in those who are learning from him.

Earlier we noted that one of the distinctive features of teaching is the wide range of methods available to the teacher. We shall now mention, in brief, five of the many methods that are available to the earnest teacher of God's Word. They are:

First, THE LECTURE METHOD. This is the oldest and most widely used of all teaching methods. This method allows the teacher to present the greatest amount of material in the least amount of time. It is also more likely to stay on the subject than are some of the methods which make use of wider participation. The DOWNSIDE of this method is that it can be the driest of all teaching methods when employed by the inexperienced or unenthusiastic teacher.

Second, THE QUESTION AND ANSWER METHOD. This method is good for stimulating the thinking of the pupils, provided the right kind of questions are asked. This method has the advantage of offering pupils the opportunity for direct and immediate response. The DOWNSIDE is that it can be very frustrating for the teacher, and also for the student, especially if the response shows a lack of understanding of the subject matter by either the student or the teacher.

Third, DISCUSSION AND DEBATE. These methods are particularly applicable to subject matter that deals with two opposite but fairly balanced points of view. For DISCUSSION, no one should begin by expressing a positive conclusion. The emphasis is upon group thinking and the attempt to progress together toward fuller understanding. In DEBATE, each side has a committed position to defend, and presents every possible point in favor of its assigned point of view.

Fourth, THE ASSIGNMENT AND REPORT method.This method is especially useful where a class contains persons who are, themselves, capable of useful teaching. This method allows for each student to prepare and present factual, devotional, or other material coordinated with lesson objects.

Fifth, THE PROJECT method. This method consists of work activity which may be done separately by each individual or by the group as a whole. The difficulty of the project depends largely upon the age group involved with the project.

Herman Harrell Horne, in his book, **"Jesus, The Master Teacher,"** points out that any teaching situation always contains at least six basic considerations: In short, they are:

1) One or more teachers.

2) One or more pupils.

3) An environment (the physical circumstances where the teaching takes place).

4) A curriculum (the material or lesson taught).

5) One or more aims (the purpose or result toward which the teacher is working).

6) One or more methods (the means used to achieve the aims).

In summary, **good teaching consists of two important things.** They are:

A) Having something worthwhile to teach, and,

B) Getting results in teaching it.

The good teacher must:
A) Be patient;
B) Be regular in attendance;
C) Have a vision that extends beyond one lesson; he must see a quarter, or a year at a time.

The greatest plus factor of Christian Education is that it teaches people to not only know the truth of the Word, but to know "THE TRUTH" — Jesus Christ, the one who is the embodiment of all that is true in the highest sense.

Therefore, **RISE TO THE CHALLENGE** OF CHRISTIAN TEACHING and strive to do it with such vigor that each person who sits under your instruction will be touched by the Spirit of God, and will endeavor to touch God for themselves.

CHAPTER NINE
THE CHALLENGE OF FASTING

Let us first take a brief look at the meaning of the words **"fasting,"** or **"to fast."** Once this has been established we shall endeavor to comprehend if it is Scriptural for the church today, if it serves any purpose, and whether there are certain people who should or should not engage in such a practice.

The MODERN GLOBE dictionary defines a **'fast'** as a "time of eating little or no food." e.g. as a religious duty or in protest.

WORLD'S BIBLE DICTIONARY states, "fasting was a common practice among the Israelites in both the Old and New Testament eras. People went without food or drink for a period, usually for a religious purpose. It may have been to express sorrow (1 Samuel 31:13; 1 Kings 21:27; Nehemiah 1:4), repentance (1 Samuel 7:6; Joel 2:12; Daniel 9:3,4), or sincerely in prayer (2 Chronicles 20:3,4; Ezra 8:23).

According to W. E. Vine the GREEK verb NESTEUO which is closely related to the noun means "to fast, to abstain from eating and is used of voluntary fasting" (Matthew 4:2; 6: 16-18; 9:14, 15; Mark 2:18-20; Luke 5:33-35; 18:12; Acts 13: 2, 3). Some of these passages show that teacher's to whom scholars or disciples were attached, gave them special instructions as to fasting. Christ taught the need of purity and simplicity of motive.

Mr. Vine continues to say, "the answers of Christ to the questions of the disciples of John and of the Pharisees reveal His whole purpose and method. No doubt He and His followers observed such a Fast as that on the Day of Atonement, but He imposed no frequent fasts in addition. What He taught was suitable to the change of character and purpose which He designed for His disciples. His claim to be the Bridegroom, Matthew 9:15 and the reference there to the absence of fasting, virtually involved a claim to be the Messiah" (cf. Zechariah 8:19).

The only official fast according to the Jewish law was the annual DAY OF ATONEMENT (assuming that 'to afflict yourselves' means 'to fast'—Leviticus 23:27). The Jews later introduced a series of FASTS to mourn the destruction of Jerusalem by Babylon in 587 B. C. (Zechariah 8:19). Because of the association of **fasting with mourning,** Jesus' disciples did not fast while He was with them. THAT WAS A TIME OF JOY! They fasted only when He was taken from them and killed; but their sorrow was turned into joy at His resurrection. Luke 5:33-35 says, "And they said unto Him, Why do the disciples of John fast often, and make prayers, and likewise the disciples of the Pharisees; but Thine eat and drink? And He said unto them, Can ye make the children (friends of the Bridegroom) of the bride-chamber fast, while the bridegroom is with them? But the days will come, when the bridegroom shall be taken away from them, and then shall they fast in those days."

Both the Old and New Testaments speak of those who fasted insincerely. Certain people made a show of their fasting, thinking that they were impressing others, and in particular impressing God, but they were only inviting God's condemnation. Isaiah 58:3-5 says, "Wherefore have we fasted, say they, and thou seest not? Wherefore have we afflicted our soul, and thou takest no knowledge? Behold, in the day of your fast you find pleasure, and exact (exploit) all your labors (laborers). Behold, ye fast for strife and debate, and to smite (strike) with the fist of wickedness: ye shall not fast as ye do this day, to make your voice to be heard on high. Is it such a fast that I have chosen? A day for a man to afflict his soul? Is it to bow down his head as a bulrush, and to spread sackcloth and ashes under him? Wilt thou call this a fast, and an acceptable day to the Lord?" Matthew 6:16-18, "Jesus said, Moreover when ye fast, be not, as the hypocrites (pretenders), of a sad countenance: for they disfigure their faces, that they may appear unto men to fast. Verily I say unto you, They have their reward. But thou, when thou fastest, anoint thine head, and wash thy face; that thou appear not unto men to fast, but unto thy Father Who is in secret: and thy Father, Who is in secret, shall reward thee openly."

In the gospel of Luke, verses 11 and 12 is the story of the Pharisee, who boasted in all that he did, as well as in his fasting, thinking that this was going to benefit or gain him merit with the Lord. As the story unfolds the person who went home changed and justified was the poor sinner who had nothing to boast about. He simply put his trust in his Lord and received a new life. By contrast to the Pharisee and others who make a pretense in fasting, God approves of true fasting, whether individually or collectively, when it was combined with genuine prayer. Matthew 4:1-4, "Then was

Jesus led up of the Spirit into the wilderness to be tempted of the devil. And when **He had fasted** forty days and forty nights, He was afterward an hungered (hungry). And when the tempter came to Him, he said, If thou be the Son of God, command that these stones be made bread. But He (Jesus) answered and said, It is written, Man shall not live by bread alone, but by every word that proceedeth out of the mouth of God." Luke 2:37, "And she (Anna) was a widow of about fourscore and four years, which departed not from the temple, but served God with fastings and prayers night and day." Acts 13: 2, 3, "And they ministered to the Lord, and fasted, and the Holy Ghost said, Separate me Barnabas and Saul for the work whereunto I have called them. And when they had fasted and prayed, and laid their hands on them, they sent them away."

The Bible gives no explanation of the practical purpose of fasting but examples of fasting in the New Testament show that it often accompanied prayer when people faced unusually difficult tasks or decisions, or met unusually strong opposition from Satan. The **purpose of the fast** may have been to separate the person as much as possible from the common affairs of everyday life. This would enable him, without distraction, to concentrate all of his spiritual powers on the important issues before him.

WORLD'S BIBLE dictionary has covered the purpose of the fast for the disciples in the New Testament but WHAT ABOUT THIS PRESENT AGE? Does the same purpose hold water for the disciples of Christ today? The answer in a word is **'YES.'**

We, in North America, may not suffer the same physical persecution as did the early disciples. I am sure that we do not suffer persecution such as that which our brothers and sisters suffer in countries with dictatorial and communist rulership. We do, however, suffer mental anguish, discrimination, and mockery from the enemies of Christ. A little while ago a person on the television show, *"Politically Incorrect,"* said that anyone who believes in any kind of religion, especially Christians, is mentally retarded. Because of these enemies of the Cross of Christ and the gospel, the child of God should spend time in FASTING to gain spiritual power to overcome all temptation and be strong in the Lord (Ephesians 6:10).

If we learn to deny the body its natural food, at specific time periods, bringing it into subjection, this will help us to discipline our lives so as to concentrate on the issues that face us. For example, many of the Hollywood stars 'fast' when doing movies because they feel that to do so sharpens their mind and thinking processes. How much more will fasting help the children of God sharpen their spiritual mind to hear and understand what the Lord says to the church!

Another purpose of fasting is to draw near to God, not so much to gain His approval as to experience His power upon our life. The Bible says, "Draw near to God, and He will draw near to you." Of course, when we fast for this purpose WE MUST COUPLE IT WITH PRAYER, for that is how we communicate with the Lord.

A NOTE OF CAUTION CONCERNING FASTING. To fast for any purpose is to open oneself up to receive either from the Lord or from the enemy. Therefore, when we fast, we must at all time be in the attitude and spirit of prayer so as to receive from the good hand of God. I have had folk say to me, "Pastor, I would like to fast but I cannot do it because I have sugar diabetes or some other illness." Let me say to you, "Be of good cheer"—God knows the attitude of your heart. That's what is important in His sight. You will be rewarded for having a heart that yearns for God, not for fasting, because even though you cannot fast, you spend time in His presence in prayer. We saw from the Scriptures that God is more concerned with the attitude of the heart than whether or not you fast, or any other physical action. It is man that looks at the outward appearance (what you do). God looks at the inner man.

However, there are others who have no physical illness, yet should not fast. WHO ARE THEY? They are the ones who fast for selfish reasons or with incorrect motives. Remember the man who boasted that he fasted twice in the week, that he was not like that Publican, etc. His motives were wrong and he did not receive forgiveness. The Publican did not fast at all, yet he received forgiveness and went home justified (just as if he never sinned). Those who fast with wrong motives cannot expect to receive from the Lord because all they have done is open themselves up for a demonic attack. When we fast we must do so out of a pure heart, with a focus on Christ, so as to experience His power and be better able to serve Him.

There are several different types or kinds of fasts mentioned in the Bible. We would refer to them as either 'partial' or 'complete' fasts. One person may feel a leading to go on a complete fast, without food or water, for a period of time. Moses did this twice for forty days each time, Jesus also did it after His baptism in the Jordan River. Others may fast sweets for a period of time. Still others may fast meats, and so on.

Regardless of the kind of fast you attempt, keep in mind to pray during that period. The length of time for your fast is between you and God—no one can instruct another on how long a fast should be or even whether a certain person should or should not fast. These are private matters between each individual and his Lord.

Seeing that fasting is interwoven throughout the Bible, I believe that it is as Scriptural to fast NOW as it was for the early disciples.

The Apostle Paul said, "to approve yourselves in fasting." Again, to the Corinthian believers he said, "give yourselves to fasting and prayer…" 1 Corinthians 7:5. In speaking with His disciples, Jesus assured them that certain kinds of demonic spirits come out only as a result of prayer and fasting. Matthew 17:21, "Howbeit this kind goeth not out but by prayer and fasting." This says a lot about the value of fasting and if Jesus has not changed (Hebrews 13:8), I am confident that Satan has not changed either. Therefore, if certain spirits were cast out only by prayer and fasting when Jesus walked on earth it is no doubt that the same is true of the day in which we live.

IT IS SURELY A CHALLENGE to deny oneself of the basic necessities of food so as to have the power of God upon ones life, but it is worth it. Remember, that you cannot earn or merit God's power or anointing, but by fasting you are saying, "Lord, I deny my flesh so that you might have the preeminence in my life. I want you to be in control. I place myself into subjection to you, and to your will for my life." James 4:7 says, "Submit yourself therefore to God; resist the devil and he will flee from you." Pray that God will give you wisdom and understanding as you face THE CHALLENGE OF FASTING for your life and ministry. YOU CAN DO IT!!!

CHAPTER TEN
THE CHALLENGE OF FACING THE ENEMY

In failing the temptation of a seductive young woman, one man stated that he was not fit for much good because he "saw the varmint." To him the "varmint" was an illicit affair that he could not resist.

Pastor, Christian worker, what is the "varmint" (enemy) that troubles your life? To face that thing does not mean to succumb to it. Rather, it means to conquer or overcome the thing so that it is no longer an enemy that can defeat you. Remember, with Christ in the vessel, you can smile at the storm. Jesus said, "I give unto you power against all the power of the enemy, and nothing shall by any means hurt you."

The enemies to the work of the Lord does not include mockers, scoffers, and persecutors, only. They also include greed, lust, bitterness, illicit sexual acts, and so on. **The question remains:** Are you FACING THE CHALLENGE OF THE ENEMY in your life, or are you trying to hide your head in the sand hoping that the thing will go away? I have news for you—**IT WON'T GO AWAY!** You have to face it down, deal with it, and overcome it, so as to live in victory. YOU CAN DO IT with the help of the Lord and with the power of His Word. Philippians 4:13 says, "I can do all things through Christ who strengthens me."

Dear reader, you need to say that, over and over again, until it gets into your spirit. When your spirit gets a hold on this it will direct your intellect so that your intellect will come in line with the Word. When that happens your life will be revolutionized. Repeat the words: "I can, I can do, I can do all things, I can do all things through Christ." WHY? "Because He gives me strength." Maybe you remember the story of the little train that you learned when you were a child. It was trying to go up a long, steep hill and was finding it very difficult. As it went along, it kept repeating, "I think I can, I think I can, I think I can." After it reached the summit and began to go down the other side it began to say, "I thought I could, I thought I could, I thought I could." Are you getting the message? You say, "But I am so weak." The Bible says, "When I am weak, then am I strong because the strength of God comes to us and makes us strong in Him," II Corinthians 12:10. When we are weak in our own strength or ability, then we let God and His Word work through us and we become strong in Him and in the power of His might. Ephesians 6:10, "Finally, my brethren, be strong in the Lord, and in the power of His might."

The ultimate enemy of the child of God is none other than that old serpent, Satan. John 10:10 says, "The thief (enemy, referring to Satan) cometh not but for to kill, to steal, and to destroy." Please notice that this enemy of the soul comes for three distinct purposes which are: **First,** to kill; **Second,** to steal; **Third,** to destroy. In other words, he comes to kill your joy, steal your happiness (witness), and ultimately destroy your soul. All other enemies of the child of God are directly or indirectly connected to the ultimate enemy of the soul, Satan. However, Satan and all of his off-spring can be overcome by two things. **First,** the blood of the Lamb (Jesus); **Second,** the word of your testimony (Revelation 12:11).

THE BLOOD OF THE LAMB:

In the Old Testament only the high priest could enter into the Holy of Holies (beyond the veil, the holiest of all), and only once each year, to offer sacrifices for himself and for the errors (sins) of the people (Hebrews 9:7) to secure their pardon for another year. Note the words of the above Scripture, "But into the second went the high priest alone once every year, not without blood, which he offered for himself, and for the errors (sins committed in ignorance) of the people. 8) The Holy Ghost this signifying, that the way into the holiest of all was not yet made manifest, while the first tabernacle was yet standing." Every time a sin was committed, as well as at other times, and for other reasons, a sacrifice was to be offered and blood sprinkled. But there came a time when the blood of bulls and goats could no longer be sufficient to secure the pardon and forgiveness of the people. The Lord desired to have a **'once for all'** sacrifice that not only would cover the people's sins for a year, but would take them away altogether. Hence, when John the Baptist saw Jesus coming to him to be baptized, he exclaimed, "Behold the Lamb of God, Who takes away the sins of the world" (John 1:29).

One of the GREATEST CHALLENGES for a minister

of the gospel is to preach the "blood of Jesus Christ, God's Son, cleanseth from all sin and all unrighteousness." This is not a popular subject in these end times. It is considered a negative gospel. Let me be emphatic in declaring that it is this negative aspect of the gospel that gives us the positive side of the gospel, which is everlasting life, divine healing, a home in heaven, etc. NOTE, that it is the blood that maketh an atonement for the soul, because "without the shedding of blood, there is no remission (forgiveness) of sins," Hebrews 9:22.

QUESTION: How are you going to face your enemy? Let me encourage you to face him without fear because of the blood of the Lamb, Jesus Christ.

David said to Goliath, "You come to me with spear and armor, but I come to you in the name of the Lord." Because of the blood of Christ being applied to your heart, you, too, can face your giant in the name of the Lord, and when you do so in submission to His will, your giant (whatever it may be) will have to flee (James 4:7).

THE WORD OF YOUR TESTIMONY:

The Bible says, "For by thy words thou shalt be justified, and by thy words thou shalt be condemned," Matthew 12: 37. "Death and life are in the power of the tongue:....," Proverbs 18:21. "I call heaven and earth to record (as witnesses) this day against you, that I have set before you life and death, blessing and cursing: therefore choose life, that both thou and thy seed (children) may live," Deuteronomy 30:19. These Scriptures alone conclude that we can choose what our testimony is going to be. We can choose whether we will have a positive,

God-honoring, people-building testimony or whether we will have a negative, complaining, testimony that no one wants to be around. How are you going to let the world see Christ portrayed in your testimony. The CHOICE is YOURS!! A testimony that is negative, whining, and complaining about everything with an 'I can't' in front of it is one that is a failure. NOTE THAT GOD SAYS, "Let your yea (yes) be yea (yes); and your no, no. Anything more than that is sin."

The Psalmists' testimony was that he slew a lion and a bear, so who does this uncircumcised Philistine (Goliath) think he is that he can defy the armies of the living God of Israel and get away with it. Refer back to our introduction as found in 1 Samuel 17. David stood his ground against this enemy of the children of God because he knew the power of his God. He knew that His God would deliver him. If you knew nothing more than deliverance from sin and a new life in Christ, that should be enough to make you stand up and **RISE TO THE CHALLENGE** OF THE ENEMY, and face him down in the name of Jesus Christ.

The Apostle Paul said, "I am not ashamed of the gospel of Christ, for it is the power of God unto salvation" (Romans 1:16). Because of this confident testimony of the power of the grace of Christ and what it could do for the sinner this same Apostle of Christ could later say without fear or doubt "I know whom I have believed and am persuaded that He is able to keep that which I have committed unto Him against that day."

When we have such an assurance, we will overcome every force of wickedness that rises against us. We will rise against it and be victorious through Jesus Christ.

Remember Philippians 4:13? "I can do all things through Christ which strengthens me." 1 John 5:4 says, "This is the victory that overcomes the world, even our faith." A testimony of being cleansed by the blood of Christ, accepted into the beloved, and walking by the faith of Christ will give us the stamina, the will, the courage, and the power to overcome every mountain that stands in our way. The prophet Isaiah states in chapter 54, verse 17 that, "No weapon that is formed against thee shall prosper; and every tongue that shall rise against thee in judgment (condemnation) thou shalt condemn. This is the heritage of the saints of the Lord, and their righteousness is of me, saith the Lord."

The Lord said to JOSHUA in chapter 1, verses 6 and 8, "Be strong, and of a good courage; be not afraid, nor be dismayed; for I am thy God, I will be with thee." He also commanded Joshua to, "meditate upon His law day and night, to not let it depart out of his mouth and the Lord would make his way prosperous and give him good success." Joshua had confidence that God would help him as he led the people of the Lord into the Promised Land. That is a tremendous testimony, to have the kind of faith or confidence that whatever comes your way you will trust the Lord. If the Lord said it, you can count on it. He will not fail but will perform His word. He said, "My word shall not return unto me void, (empty, without fruit) but it shall accomplish that which I please, and it shall prosper in the thing whereto I sent it" (Isaiah 55:11).

In the New Testament Paul states, "...., whatsoever things are true, whatsoever things are honest, whatsoever things are just, whatsoever things are pure, whatsoever things are lovely, whatsoever things are of good report; if there be any virtue, and if there be any praise, think on these things" (Philippians 4:8). If we do these things we shall have a testimony that will be pleasing in God's sight, and we will overcome every CHALLENGE that the enemy puts before us. NOTE that before Enoch was translated to heaven he had a testimony that he pleased God. Hebrews 11:5, "By faith Enoch was translated that he should not see death; and was not found, because God took him: for before his translation he had this testimony, that he pleased God." It seems to me that if we do not have a testimony that is pleasing in the sight of the Lord we will not be translated into the presence of the Lord. Once again, "They overcame by the blood of the Lamb, and the word of their testimony" (Revelation 12:11).

As a minister to ministers, as a servant to servants, I challenge you to overcome any hindrance that may be in your life, whether past or present. One writer put it this way, "Get past your past." I CHALLENGE YOU, RISE UP AND MEET THE ENEMY OF PAST EXPERIENCE, defeat it and let it go—It's behind you. There's nothing you can do to change what has happened. Paul said, "Forgetting those things which are behind, I press (reach, stretch) forward toward the goal, for the prize of the high calling of God in Christ Jesus" (Philippians 3:14). Therefore, if you cannot change the past—forget the past! It's gone! Rather than dwelling upon and feeling guilty about what is gone, look toward the future with high expectations for a bright and glorious time in the Lord. Remember, the future is as bright as the promises of God!

As you read these words, you may be one of the thousands who are saying that you just cannot get over some dreadful thing that happened in your life. As a result, you bring the guilt of the past into the present and project it into the future, thereby seeing nothing for the future except gloom, despair, dejection, fear and loneliness. WHAT AN AWFUL NEGATIVE TRAP TO BE CAUGHT INTO! That is the snare (trap) of the enemy to keep you from walking and living in the victory that Jesus Christ won for you at Calvary.

Beloved, I have good news for you. The Bible states, "There is therefore now no condemnation (guilt feelings about the past) to those who are in Christ Jesus..." (Romans 8:1). Again, "As far as the east is from the west, so far hath He removed your transgressions from you" (Psalm 103:12), and "The blood of Jesus Christ, God's Son, cleanseth from all sin and all unrighteousness" (1 John 1:7, 9).

Upon the basis of the above Scriptures and promises of God, (there are many others), turn your negatives into positives; turn your sorrow into joy; your guilt into happiness; and your frustration into peace and contentment. Let your testimony be changed from gloom and despair to "I can do all things through Christ....." and "My God shall supply all your need...."

RISE TO THE CHALLENGE, put the enemy under your feet, and walk in the victory that Christ has won for you. God said, "I will make you the head and not the tail, you shall be above and not beneath." Remember, Christ is the Victor and we, in Him are victors, not victims. We will not be defeated, we will not become disheartened, because we are "more than conquerors through Christ Jesus the Lord" (Romans 8:37). The giant will fall as you MEET THE CHALLENGE in the name of the Lord.

CHAPTER ELEVEN
THE CHALLENGE OF FACING REALITY
(present and future)

Reality means: a) the state of being real; b) something which is real or exists in fact.

In almost every situation or circumstance people seem to go through a period of denial before they face the reality of that particular thing. They not only deny the reality of the problem but when they finally realize that the problem must be faced they procrastinate as long as possible to avoid facing it.

For one to accomplish something in life, whether in the spiritual realm or the physical realm, whether in the Christian realm or the secular realm, he must not deny the reality of problems or procrastinate in solving them. Rather, he must accept life's problems and injustices as a CHALLENGE and use them as stepping stones to become all that he can be.

God's people cannot, and will not, advance and become great without seeing problems as stepping stones which can be used to move to a higher level. For example, a person may for many years feel like opening a business. However, he knows that there are many pitfalls and he may not succeed. He has a good job, so why face the unknown. His job is secure, or, so he thinks, until one day he is called into the office and told that at the end of the month the company is closing. This person can do one of two things: **First,** he can deny the reality of the situation that faces him until the day that it actually happens and he is thrust out into the cold, harsh world without employment; or, **Second,** he can face the problem as presented to him and ACCEPT it as A CHALLENGE to open his own business. If his business fails, it fails—he didn't have a job to begin with. But what if his business prospers. Are you getting the message?

The person faces the reality, ACCEPTS THE CHALLENGE, and in time becomes a prosperous business person. He used the reality of losing his job as a stepping stone to greatness. IS THAT NOT WHAT GOD WANTS FOR HIS PEOPLE?

Facing reality may mean having to move to another town. Don't look at that as a problem, view it as a challenge to meet new people, make new friends, and win souls to Christ. Of course, it is difficult, but don't set your heart upon the difficulty—set your heart upon the One Who has called you, Jesus Christ. **He is the all-sufficient One!**

How do you face the CHALLENGE OF THE FUTURE? I want to show you four ways to face the future. There are others but if you face it in the four following ways you will be victorious in your daily living. Why the future? Because reality dictates that we face the future with its inherent problems just as we face the present with its problems. We cannot run or hide from it—therefore we must face it. It is true that we do not know what the future holds but we know who holds the future and so we take courage and walk into the unknown of tomorrow with the Christ of God who has won all our victories for us, in advance.

Deuteronomy 31:8 says, "And the Lord, He it is Who goes before you; He will be with you, He will not fail you, neither forsake you: fear not, neither be dismayed." Beloved, this verse tells you that God goes before you. WHY? To make the way straight for you to walk in. The mountains He makes into plains, and the crooked places He makes straight.

He not only goes before you but He will also be with you in the power of His Spirit. Jesus said, "I will not leave you, nor forsake you," and, "Lo, I am with you to the end." Speaking through His prophet, God said that everything we do and everywhere we go is done by the Spirit of the Lord and not in our own strength or power. Note the words, "Not by might (of man), nor by power (human attainment), but by My Spirit, saith the Lord of hosts." Not only does He go before you and be with you, but He will not fail you. WHAT A BEAUTIFUL PROMISE! Others will fail and let you down. Even your best friend, your parents, and even your pastor may fail you, but Hebrews 13:8 says, "Jesus Christ is the same (never changing) yesterday, today, and forever." He is well able to perform that which He has spoken. He will not fail!

One song writer put it this way, *"Because He lives, I can face tomorrow; Because He lives ALL fear is gone; Because I know He holds the future, my life is worth living, just because He lives."* Yes, dear reader, because Jesus is alive and because God made the above promises, you can FACE

THE CHALLENGE OF THE FUTURE without fear, dismay or discouragement.

NOTE: The four ways to face the reality of the future are: 1) with confidence; 2) with commitment; 3) with cheerfulness; and 4) with courage.

First, face the future with confidence. Philippians 1:6 says, "Being confident of this very thing, that He which hath begun a good work in you will perform (complete) it until the day of Jesus Christ." The world is filled with violence, turmoil and trouble, and many face the future with a sense of frustration and doubt. They are so unsure of what the future may hold for them. There seems to be no use trying because they just can't overcome or get ahead in life. Even many of God's children, and ministers in particular, throw in the towel, so to speak, with an overwhelming sense of frustration and hopelessness. They thought they were going to change the world but found that they can't do it. They see this as defeat and failure in the mirror of life. Their eyes are focused in the rear view mirror and, as a result, all that can be seen is what was. These past defeats are then brought into the present where they still live in defeat or misery and guilt about not doing better. This is then projected into the future where all that can be seen is more of the same. Little wonder so many pastors quit the ministry and get a secular job. It is not easy to be a pastor but if God has called you, get back to your calling. Do not give up! There is victory just ahead! Face the reality of defeats and use them as stepping stones to a greater ministry.

Beloved, you need to CHANGE YOUR OUTLOOK on life so as to live in victory now, and see victory for the future. The Apostle Paul said, "This one thing I do, forgetting those things which are behind, I press forward….." How do you change your outlook? **First, forget the past**—you can't change it, so forget it and move on. **Second,** change your negative thinking for positive thinking. As a child of God, you should always have a positive outlook on life. Philippians 4:8 says, "….Whatsoever things are true, whatsoever things are honest, whatsoever things are just, whatsoever things are pure, whatsoever things are lovely, whatsoever things are of good report; if there be any virtue, and if there be any praise, think on these things." This verse of Scripture states the prerequisite for experiencing the peace of God and freedom from anxiety, which is made abundantly clear from verse 9: "If you do these things, the God of peace shall be with you." Again, "Thou wilt keep him in perfect peace whose mind is stayed on Thee: because he trusteth in Thee" (Isaiah 26:3). This is the confidence that we can have in Him Who never slumbers, sleeps, makes mistakes, or fails. **Third,** change your outlook by changing your up-look. When trouble abounds on every hand, "look up and lift up your head, for your redemption draweth near." David said, "I will look unto the hills. From whence cometh my help? My help cometh from the Lord." Your help is not in your own strength. You will find it in the Lord Jesus Christ. Psalm 37:3 says, "Trust in the Lord, and do good; so shalt thou dwell in the land, and verily thou shalt be fed." Literally, "have confidence in God, do good; and you will then feed on His faithfulness." WHY? Because He is faithful and will give victory to those who call upon Him in the day of their distress.

Second, face the future with commitment. Psalm 37:5 says, "Commit your way unto the Lord; trust also in Him, and He shall bring it to pass."

James 4:7 states, "Submit yourselves therefore to God. Resist the devil and he will flee from you." When I was a boy, testimony services were common place in the church. They were a part of the worship service and no church service was complete without one. During those times of sharing one would often hear stories told that just did not come out right. One man, in particular, would always quote the last part of James 4:7, "Resist the devil and he will flee from you." One day I confronted this old gentleman, in a very nice way, and told him that the Bible doesn't say it just like that. Rather than be offended at what I had said, he asked, *"What does it say then?"* I proceeded to tell him that the devil is not afraid of us nor will he flee from us unless we adhere to the first part of the verse which states that we are to be submissive to the will of God in our lives. Jesus said, "Not my will, but Thine be done. Not as I will, but as thou wilt." If Jesus had to be submissive to the will of the Father, how much more ought we to be submissive to His divine will.

Beloved, you can resist the devil from now until eternity and he will not flee (run) from you unless and until you have completely committed and submitted yourself to the Lordship of Christ.

COMMITMENT MEANS SACRIFICE. It means you are sold out to what you believe. You are committed to a cause and nothing or no one can sway you from that cause.

To commit your way unto the Lord is to say that you want your will to be lost in His. It is to say with the Apostle Paul, "I am crucified with Christ: nevertheless, I live; yet not I, but Christ liveth in me: and the life which I now live in the flesh I live by the faith of the Son of God,

Who loved me, and gave Himself for me" (Galatians 2:20). It is also to say with the Lord Jesus, "…: nevertheless, not as I will, but as Thou wilt" (Matthew 26:39). Jesus was committed to giving His life as a ransom for lost humanity and nothing could alter that commitment.

To the ministers reading these words, let me encourage you in your commitment to FACE THE REALITY AND CHALLENGE OF THE FUTURE with confidence, cheerfulness and courage. **Hold on!!** You will be victorious! The Lord promised that He would bring His will to pass in your life if you commit your way to Him. Don't try to face the challenges of life in your own strength—you will fail. Face them in the strength of the Spirit and say with the Apostle Paul, "I can do all things through Christ, Who strengthens me" (Philippians 4:13).

To the Roman believers Paul wrote, "I beseech you by the mercies of God to present your bodies a living sacrifice unto God, holy, and acceptable, which is your reasonable service" (Romans 12:1). This is to say that to face the future with commitment, we must be completely, unreservedly, yielded to the will of God, and be dependent upon His infinite wisdom and power to help us overcome. He is really saying, "Look what the Lord has done for you. He saved you, He washed you in His own blood, healed your sicknesses, therefore I am not asking you to do something unreasonable, but to simply commit yourself completely into the care of the Lord."

Child of God, if you feel broken, worn-out, and can't go on, make that new commitment to the challenge and watch your life change from defeat to victory in Jesus

Christ. I promise you that you will want to get up and start going again in the name of the Lord.

Third, face the future with cheerfulness. Psalm 37:4, "Delight thyself also in the Lord: and He shall give thee the desires of thine heart."

The writers of the FULL LIFE STUDY BIBLE state, "To delight yourself in the Lord is to desire and enjoy the nearness of His presence and the truth and righteousness of His Word, (cf. Job 22:26; 27:10; Isaiah 58:14). To those who delight themselves in the Lord, God gives the desires of their hearts. **One,** God will answer the cry of our hearts if our desires are in accord with His will. **Two,** when we delight ourselves in God and His will, God Himself places desires within our hearts that He then sets out to fulfill."

The definition of "delight" as given in the *FUNK AND WAGNALLS DICTIONARY* is:1) great pleasure; gratification; joy; 2) that which gives extreme pleasure; 3) the quality of delighting; charm; 4) rejoice.

MATTHEW HENRY states, "We must make God our heart's delight and then we shall have our heart's desire. We were commanded (v.3) to do good, and then follows this command to delight in God, which is as much a privilege as a duty. And this present duty has a promise annexed to it, *"He shall give thee the desires of thine heart."* He has not promised to gratify all the appetites of the body, but to grant all the desires of the heart, all the cravings of the soul. What is the desire of the heart of a good man? It is this, to know, and love, and live to God, to please Him and to be pleased in Him.

To be cheerful, happy, excited, one must not look back or dwell upon the negatives of life of which there are many. At times, it seems that the negatives are more and greater than the positives and, as a result, many of God's children dwell upon the bad situations. If you live in and are surrounded by negativity, you will likely view life as a negative, thereby living a miserable existence. GOD DOES NOT WISH THIS FOR HIS PEOPLE. Jesus said, "I have come that they might have life and have it more abundantly" (John 10:10).

God wants His people to be a positive, cheerful people who will live life as a challenge—something to be conquered and enjoyed. The life of Christ ought to shine through us like the sun shining through the clouds as they break apart. The love, joy and warmth of God's Spirit should cause us to have a smile on our face, even in the most adverse circumstances. The Apostle Paul faced much adversity but he had such assurance of the love of God that he could say, "Rejoice in the Lord always, (not some of the time, but always), and again, I say rejoice" (Philippians 4:4).

Job went through much adversity in life. He lost his children, his cattle, his finances, his health, and in essence, his wife because she told him to curse God and die. Job did not call a pity party to lament the negative side of things in life. Instead, he told his wife that she talked like a foolish woman and that yes, he would maintain his integrity before his God. WHY? Because he could see the positive side—he didn't bring anything into this world and it was certain that he could take nothing out. His attitude was, "If I live, I live; If I die, I die." One thing is for certain, "I know that my redeemer is alive and after the skin worms destroy this body, yet in my flesh shall I see God" (Job 19:25, 26). He remained cheerful and faced his future with a positive outlook because he knew his God. As a result, Job had more at the end than he did at the beginning. WHAT A WONDERFUL TESTIMONY TO THE GRACE AND PROVIDENCE OF GOD!!

My friend, no matter what may come your way, "be steadfast, unmovable, always abounding (excelling) in the work of the Lord" (1 Corinthians 15:58). It is indeed A CHALLENGE TO FACE THE REALITY OF THE FUTURE, always looking for the good, in the midst of a crooked and perverse generation, but God is on your side. He will not fail, so, look up, your deliverance is drawing near.

Fourth, face the future with courage. Philippians 1:20 says, "According to my earnest expectation and hope, that in nothing I shall be ashamed, but that with all boldness, as always, so now also Christ shall be magnified in my body, whether it be by life, or by death."

If you read through the life story of the Apostle Paul, you will find that he was beaten with a cat-o-nine tails (stripes) three times; he was shipwrecked on an open ocean; he was stoned and left for dead; he should have died at the bite of a venomous viper; he spent much of his Christian life in prison, from which he did his greatest writing. If someone had reason to be discouraged and give up, this man did. Like Job, he knew the end. He could see the *'Pot of Gold'* at the end of the rain-bow, so to speak. Therefore, he took courage and faced the future with it because God was his source. NOTE Paul's words, "For to me, to live is Christ, and to die is gain" (Philippians 1: 21). "Who shall separate us from the love of Christ? Shall tribulation, or distress, or famine, or persecution, or nakedness, or peril, or sword? As it is written, 'For Thy sake we are killed all the day long; we are accounted as sheep for the slaughter.' Nay in all these things we are more than conquerors through Him that loved us. For I am persuaded, that neither death, nor life, nor angels, nor principalities, nor powers, nor things present, nor things to come, nor height, nor depth, nor any other creature, shall be able to separate us from the love of God, which is in Christ Jesus our Lord" (Romans 8:35-39). With an assurance such as this, there is no reason for us to be discouraged. We can take heart and face life just as courageously as did the Apostle Paul, and overcome in the race of life because of the power of the Spirit of God in our life.

In the book of Acts, chapter three, there was a lame man who sat at the gate of the temple. We do not know the reason for him being lame (unable to walk), but he had been this way since childbirth. One day Peter and John were about to enter the temple for prayer service and this man sat begging for alms (money). Peter and John had no money to give to him but fastening their eyes upon him said, **"look on us."** As he did they reached out, caught him by the hand, and lifted him up. He received strength in his ankle bones and was completely healed by the power of God. The Bible says that he went leaping and praising God. There were many onlookers and criticizers present which gave these two servants of God an opportunity to preach Christ.

As Peter began to preach to the people, we find that the priests, the captain of the guard, and the Sadducees came and arrested these two men of God. Acts 4:1-3, "And as they spake unto the people, the priests, and the captain of the temple, and the Sadducees, came upon them, being grieved (greatly disturbed) that they taught the people, and preached through Jesus the resurrection from the dead. And they laid hands upon them and put them in hold (custody, prison) unto the next day:...." When these leaders found that they had no real charge against Peter and John and saw their boldness they had no choice but to let them go, after threatening them and commanding them not to speak or teach anymore in the name of Jesus.

These men did not become disillusioned or discouraged by what had happened to them. Instead, as soon as they were released they went to their own company (church gathering), reported to this group what was done, and prayed for more power and boldness (courage) to go forth winning more converts and working more miracles. Acts 4:23-31, "And being let go, they went to their own company (companions), and reported all that the chief priests and elders had said unto them. And when they heard that they lifted up their voice to God with one accord, and said, Lord, Thou art God, which hast made heaven, and earth, and the sea, and all that in them is: Who by the mouth of Thy servant David hast said, Why did the heathen rage, and the people imagine (plot) vain things? The kings of the earth stood up (took their stand), and the rulers were gathered together against the Lord, and against His Christ....And now, Lord, behold their threatening: and grant unto thy servants, that with all boldness they may speak Thy Word, by stretching forth Thine hand to heal; and that signs and wonders may be done by the name of Thy holy child Jesus.... and they were all filled with the Holy Ghost, and they spake the Word of God with boldness."

Child of God, take courage in the work that you are doing for the Lord. Know your calling and pray for the enabling power of the Holy Spirit to give you the victory that you desire. He will do it! You will not be defeated as long as put your trust in the Lord. Isaiah 41:10 says, "Fear thou not; for I am with thee: be not dismayed (crushed in spirit); for I am thy God; I will strengthen thee; Yea, I will help thee; Yea, I will uphold thee with the right hand of My righteousness."

Do not run or hide from reality, face it. JERRY SAVELLE says that there are two kinds of reality—"the lesser and the greater or higher. Sickness, sin, and disease are real—but God's Word is more real. Therefore, base your life, your thoughts, your actions, your confession upon the greater reality and the lesser reality must come into submission to the greater." In other words, hide God's Word in your heart, study it, eat it, until it becomes a part of you and you become a part of it. You will then see miracles happen for you. **RISE TO THE CHALLENGE** THAT LIES BEFORE YOU IN THE NAME OF JESUS AND YOU WILL CONQUER!

Whatever life throws your way, face it because you are not a victim, you are a victor through Jesus Christ. RISE TO THE CHALLENGE, and the reality of it will be that your circumstances will become stepping stones to greater things in the Lord!

CHAPTER TWELVE
THE CHALLENGE OF CORRECTING

2 Timothy 3:16 states, "All Scripture is given by inspiration of God, and is profitable for doctrine, for reproof **for correction,** for instruction in righteousness: 17) that the man of God may be perfect, thoroughly furnished unto all good works."

The English transliteration of the GREEK word for correction as used in verse sixteen is *EPANORTHOSIS* (epi, to; ana, up, or again; and ortho, to make straight), literally, a restoration to an upright or right state. Hence, in the above verse "correction" refers to improvement of life and character.

A part of the preaching of the gospel (good news) of Christ is to correct the hearers in such a way that will not be offensive but will cause them to be restored to an upright state in God, which will bring about an improvement in their life and character. Dear reader, the gospel is good news and it changes lives.

W. E. VINE says that the word *PAIDEIA* denotes the training of a child, including instruction; hence, discipline, correction, "chastening," suggesting the Christian discipline that regulates character. Ephesians 6:4, "And, ye fathers, provoke not your children to wrath:

but bring them up in the nurture (training) and admonition of the Lord." Therefore, correction involves discipline. Again, the Bible says, "No chastening, correction, or discipline seems to be joyous while it is taking place." However, once it has taken place and the life and character begin to improve, we can see the good out of what seemed to be hard and cruel punishment. It is a challenge to use discipline, especially when it applies to adults who ought to know better than cause such problems as strife, divisions, etc. in the church.

Again the Bible says, "foolishness is bound in the heart of a child, but the rod of correction will bring it out." I am not talking about abuse. I am talking about proper correction. There is a difference and if you do not know it I would suggest that you get a good dictionary and look up the meanings of the two.

Remember that everyone is someone's child. We generally class ourselves as children, young people, adults, elders, etc. but everyone is someone's child, regardless of the age. More importantly, those who have accepted Christ as Lord of their life are ALL CHILDREN OF GOD. As in the natural realm, so in the spiritual realm. There are those who are babes in Christ, young people in Christ, and mature saints in Christ. This has nothing to do with age or how long one has been serving the Lord—this has to do with one's hunger and thirst for the things of God. "They that hunger and thirst after righteousness shall be filled" (Matthew 5:6).

Length of time serving the Lord does not make one qualify as a mature saint. I personally know people that have been serving the Lord for twenty, thirty years and more and they gripe, murmur, and complain about everything. Babies cry about things. Mature saints work their way through the problems instead of crying about them. At times they may need a little help, but they are always looking for the solution. Babies don't look for solutions. They see the problem and expect everyone else to cater to them. The writer of Hebrews 5:12 said, "For when for the time ye ought to be teachers, you have need that one teach you again which be the first principles of the oracles of God; and are become such as have need of milk, and not of strong meat."

The believers in the above verse of Scripture had known the Lord long enough that they should have been able to teach others concerning the grace, mercy, and truth of Christ. But they were still spiritual babies in the things of God. Hebrews 5:13, "For everyone that useth milk is unskillful in the Word of righteousness: for he is a babe." Therefore, exhortation and correction was needed to help them mature in their Christian walk. (cf. Hebrews 6:9-20).

As I stated earlier, it is not an easy task for a pastor to have to take any of his parishioners aside and set them straight through correction, reproof and rebuke. Nonetheless, there are instances when it must be done and if the shepherd is to lead the flock effectively, he will do what has to be done when it needs to be done. **RISE TO THE CHALLENGE**, my servant friend and God will reward you for your faithfulness.

I recall one pastorate where one of my people came to the parsonage and rebuked me because he thought that I was *'showing off'* in the church services. (I admit, I am quite demonstrative when preaching). I was forced as the shepherd of the flock to rebuke his attitude and correct him right there. I then proceeded to let him know that when he walked out my door, as far as I was concerned, the conversation never took place—it was forgotten. One month later, that same man stood before the adult Sunday school class and openly apologized for his attitude toward the pastor. Then, in the Sunday morning service he did the same thing to the entire congregation. He didn't have to do this but felt that he should. He told the congregation how that he wanted to change the pastor to be like him when it was God that wanted to change his heart to be more open to what the Spirit was doing and saying to the church.

Several months after moving away from that area, I received a letter from this brother, saying, "Thank you for not bowing to my pressure and for standing up to me. I do not know where I would have been had you not stood and corrected me as you did." I thank God for this young man that he did not take offence at correction but accepted it and now has become a wonderful minister of the gospel of Christ. Many souls have been won to the Lord under his ministry.

There are many other examples from my own years as a pastor and it has not always been easy to use the rod of correction. Children according to the flesh, can and do receive correction by their parents, teachers, etc. Yet, there are times when even they rebel against correction. A lot of adults are like children (and worse) because they want to see things their own way and are not willing to receive instruction, training, or correction to improve their conduct and behavior. However, if we are to grow in Christ, correction must be given and received.

Pastor, Christian worker, regardless of how difficult the situation may be, do not shirk your responsibility of correcting the saints when the need arises. **RISE TO THE CHALLENGE** with the love of Christ and do what must be done. You are the shepherd of the flock, the overseer, and God has placed you in your position to feed, care for, exhort, instruct, train, and correct when necessary. So, in the name of Jesus, RISE UP, TAKE THE CHALLENGE, and run with it.

Dear reader, I trust that you have not been offended by my straightforwardness and blunt manner of speaking. What I have said is from the heart. This is how I face the challenges of life and ministry. I understand that everything that I have said may not work for you. You have to find your own way of facing the challenges and I promise you that there will be more challenges to face should the Lord tarry a little while longer. How you deal with the challenges that you face will determine how victorious you are in your life and ministry.

So, I encourage you to FACE THE CHALLENGE, RISE UP TO MEET IT, with prayer and the Word of God. Look at each challenge as you would a mountain to climb. When you have conquered one mountain you will be more prepared to climb the next. But always remember that between every mountain that you climb there will be a valley to go through. This is where your strength is restored and renewed for the challenge of the next mountain climb. Are you still with me? I trust that you are because all that I want to do is to encourage you to not back down from the challenge of the giant who wishes to defeat you.

RISE TO MEET EVERY CHALLENGE IN THE NAME OF THE LORD, "putting on the whole armor of God," (cf. Ephesians 6:11-17). When you have done everything and don't know what else to do **"STAND."** You will conquer! You will win!! You will be victorious!!! WHY? Because God is on your side fighting for you. Exodus 14:14, "The Lord shall fight for you, and ye shall hold your peace (you shall be quiet)." Therefore, "stand still and see the salvation of the Lord." (cf. Exodus 14:13; 2 Chronicles 20:17).

Before closing this little book on meeting the challenges that face you in ministry I want to talk about one more challenge. There have been numerous books written on the subject but I feel that this writing would not be complete without a short reference to it and a challenge to you, my fellow servant in the Lord, to rise up, and meet this challenge also. I am talking about the CHALLENGE OF COUNSELING.

CHAPTER THIRTEEN
THE CHALLENGE OF COUNSELING

Proverbs 11:14, "Where no counsel is, the people fall: but in the multitude of counselors there is safety."

Proverbs 12:15, "The way of a fool is right in his own eyes: but he that hearkeneth unto counsel is wise."

Proverbs 13:10, "Only by pride cometh contention: but with the well advised is wisdom."

Proverbs 15:22, "Without counsel purposes are disappointed: but in the multitude of counselors they are established."

The above Scriptures point out the importance and necessity of seeking wise counsel. Let me be quick to point out that in this section we are speaking strictly of wise, godly counsel, though these words may not preface the word 'counsel' every time it is used. The reason for this type of counsel is that there have been, and are still instances of people receiving counsel that is neither wise nor godly. Allow me to show you from the Word of God just two examples of unwise, ungodly counsel and the devastating results of it.

First, There is the prophet Balaam, who had been summoned by Balak, king of Moab, to come and curse the Israelites for him (Numbers 22-31). As the story unfolds, God would intervene and change the curse into a blessing. Please note that Balaam was a mercenary prophet, self-willed, and interested in what was in it for him, yet he was famous in the land. Here is what king Balak says to Balaam, "Come now therefore, I pray thee, and curse this people; for they are too mighty for me: peradventure I shall prevail, that we may smite them, and that I may drive them out of the land: for I know that he whom thou blessest is blessed, and he whom thou cursest is cursed. And the elders of Moab and the elders of Midian departed with the rewards (diviner's fee) of divination in their hand; and they came unto Balaam, and spake unto him the words of Balak," (Numbers 22:6, 7; cf. Numbers 22:12-22). Balaam was eloquent in prophecy, but presumptuous in seeking to alter the Divine plan. In other words, he was double-minded, and here is what the Apostle Paul says of such a person in First Corinthians 10:21, "Ye cannot drink the cup of the Lord, and of devils (demons): ye cannot be partakers of the Lord's table, and of the table of devils (demons)." And James says in chapter one, verse eight, "a double minded man is unstable in all his ways." (cf. Numbers 23, 24). The result of Balaam's double mindedness was that he went home a failure as far as the curse was concerned. Peter, in describing false teachers, said they "have forsaken the right way, and are gone astray, following the way of Balaam the son of Beor (Bosor), who loved the wage of unrighteousness; but was rebuked for his iniquity: the dumb ass (donkey) speaking with man's voice forbade (restrained) the madness of the prophet" (2 Peter 2:15, 16). Jude says in verse 11, "Woe unto them!," (speaking of the characteristics of false teachers, "for they have gone in the way of Cain, and ran greedily after the error of Balaam for reward (profit)…"

When Balaam found that he could not curse that which God had blessed he gave Balak counsel that would cause Israel to sin, thereby incurring the wrath or judgment of God. This evil counsel is to what Moses referred when he says, "Have ye saved all the women alive? Behold, these caused the children of Israel, through the counsel of Balaam, to commit trespass against the Lord in the matter of Peor, and there was a plague among the congregation of the Lord," Numbers 31:15, 16. In speaking of the counsel that Balaam gave to Balak, Jesus says through John, the revelator, "I have a few things against thee, because thou hast there them that hold the doctrine of Balaam, who taught Balak to cast a stumbling block (put an enticement to sin) before the children of Israel, to eat things sacrificed unto idols, and to commit fornication (sexual immorality)," (Revelation 2: 14). Balaam gave counsel that caused a grievous sin in Israel and many of the people died as a result. That is not just bad counsel, that is counsel with devastating effects.

Second, First Kings Chapter twelve tells the story of Rehoboam, who had just been proclaimed king over Israel. Jeroboam, and all the people of Israel came to the king asking him to make the taxes and workload a little lighter for the people and they would serve the king forever.

King Rehoboam sent the people away telling them to return in three days and he would give them an answer. The king during this three day period consulted with the old men who gave him wise counsel. They said, "…If thou wilt be a servant unto this people this day, and wilt serve them, and answer them, and speak good words to them, then they will be thy servants forever" (v.7). You guessed it! Verse 8 says, "But he forsook the counsel of the old men, which they had given to him, and consulted with the young men who had grown up with him, and which stood before him."

These young men gave the king unwise, ungodly counsel which brought about the downfall of the king, the division of the kingdom, and the eventual judgment of God upon the nation. What a different picture we might have had if Rehoboam had listened to the godly counsel of the old men!

There are many examples in the Word of God of godly men seeking wise counsel and, as a result, did mighty exploits for the Lord. Such were men like David, Hezekiah, Solomon (in his early reign), the apostle Paul, and a host of others.

Pastor, Christian worker, you will face this area of ministry either as a CHALLENGE or a stumbling block. Someone once said, "If a pastor is not a counselor, he is only half a pastor." The question I put before you is, "How will you FACE THIS CHALLENGE?"

When someone asks you for counsel and you have given the best that you know how, then find that person did their own thing in spite of your counseling otherwise. HOW WILL YOU HANDLE THIS? I know what it is like to have counsel that you believe is directly from the heart of God and solidly based on Scripture rejected. I saw the destruction that came to one particular church as a direct result of the rejection of the counsel that I had given the church board. They thought I was wrong but later called me to say that they should have listened to what I had said to them.

Another pastor called me about a certain problem that he was facing in his church and asked how it should be handled, or what could be done about the situation. I gave that brother godly counsel but he rejected it. Another pastor gave him the same counsel that I had given but he again rejected it and did things his own way. As a result, this good pastor lost several families from his church. What a shame, when it could have been otherwise! HOW WOULD YOU HANDLE SUCH REJECTION? I believe that the way to do it is to always remember that not everyone will be helped by your counsel, but be thankful to God for those who accept your counsel and are helped by it.

WHO IS A COUNSELOR? He is one who gives counsel or advises (Proverbs 11:14), especially the king's advisor (2 Samuel 15:12; First Chronicles 27:33), or one of the chief men of the government (Job 3:14; Isaiah 1:26). In Mark 15:43 and Luke 23:50 the word 'counselor' designates a "council member" of the Sanhedrin. The Holy Spirit is also called *"The Counselor"* in the Revised Standard Version of the Bible in John 14:16, 26; 15:26; 16:7.

There are many and varied areas of counseling that one faces in ministry. Please note that you are a pastor, not a psychologist or psychiatrist. As a pastor, you are also a counselor with the Word of God as your guide. The emphasis and direction of your counseling must be always to point your counselee to the TRUE COUNSELOR, CHRIST JESUS, for He is the only one who can change a person's life, thereby changing that person's conduct and behavior.

As a counselor, you must be ever cautious of the language, (both spoken and portrayed through body movements), used. JAY E. ADAMS says, "Language is a characteristic of God. God spoke and creation took place. Language can be determinative; it can spell the difference between success and failure in counseling. It is with language that we think as well as talk.

By the word of Satan man sinned. By the living and written Word of God man is saved.

Language was given to man alone at creation and plays a large part in making man unique among God's creatures. By language, man is capable of sustaining meaningful relationships to God and other men. It made organized, interpretive thought possible."

Proverbs 18:20 points out that we feed ourselves, (not only others), on the words that we speak. "A man's belly shall be satisfied with the fruit of his mouth; and with the increase (produce) of his lips shall he be filled. Death and life are in the power of the tongue: and they that love it shall eat the fruit thereof."

In counseling you will have to deal with different people's feelings. We must be extremely careful that we do not offend anyone, if at all possible. Dealing with the feelings of the counselee refers to the perception by the counselee of a bodily state as pleasant or unpleasant. Proverbs 18:19 says, "A brother offended is harder to be won than a strong city: and their contentions are like the bars of a castle."

In this vital ministry of counseling you will also have to deal with the problems of attitude.

WHAT IS ATTITUDE? It is the combination of presuppositions, beliefs, convictions, and opinions that make up one's habitual stance at any given time toward a subject, person, or act. It is a mind-set that strongly influences behavior. In counseling, attitudes may be attacked and changed more directly than feelings, which in most cases can be altered only indirectly through change of attitude and action or behavior.

Behavior is responsible conduct. The term is best used to describe those activities of the whole person who may be judged by the law of God. There will not be a behavior change until there is an attitude change. A person's attitude determines his behavior.

For the pastor, areas of counseling will range from children, to youth, to seniors, and will include such areas as loss of loved ones (bereavement), sexual problems (including homosexuality, lesbianism, and other perversions or deviant behavior, etc.), marital problems, just to name a few.

The Christian counselor or pastor need not be reminded that they have been called to labor in opposition to the world, the flesh, and the devil. Their task involves not merely a struggle with flesh and blood, but also a fight against the supernatural forces of darkness. Ephesians 6:12, "For we wrestle not against flesh and blood, but against principalities, against powers, against the rulers of the darkness of this world (age), against spiritual wickedness (spiritual hosts of wickedness) in high places."

Counseling, therefore, must be understood and conducted as a spiritual battle. Hence, there is need for divine authority in counseling, and only Biblical counseling possesses such authority. The counselor, pastor, as an ordained man or woman of God, exercises the full authority for counseling that Christ gave to the organized church. First Thessalonians 5:12, 13, "And we beseech you, brethren, to know (recognize) them which labor among you, and are over you in the Lord, and admonish (instruct, counsel) you; and to esteem them very highly in love for their work's sake. And be at peace among yourselves. 14) Now we exhort (counsel) you, brethren, warn them that are unruly (insubordinate), comfort the feebleminded (fainthearted), support the weak, be patient toward all men." The counselor or pastor must consider himself a soldier of Christ engaged in spiritual warfare, when counseling. For this battle the **"full armor of God"** alone is sufficient.

Pastor, Christian worker, I have only high lighted the necessity of this tremendous work, but I trust that it is enough to CHALLENGE you to become involved in this great work of changing lives for Christ. The field is ripe unto harvest but the laborers are few. People are hurting and being hurt. They need someone to whom they can turn for help, someone who will not betray their confidence, someone who will listen and offer suggestions. Will you **RISE TO THE CHALLENGE** and become that person, that counselor that God would have you be? There will be periods of disappointment but the joy, happiness, satisfaction, and fulfillment in helping others become fruitful and live victorious lives will far outweigh any disappointment that you experience. You will be blessed as you allow the Lord to work through you to help others overcome the battles of life.

Remember that all counseling is not the same. There must be different techniques employed for different people. You may counsel one person with great success while failing with another. Also, should you use the same technique, it may work with one counselee but not with another. Should you find that a certain technique is not working don't be afraid to change it—this may mean the difference between success and failure. No one wants to lose someone they are trying to help but it does occasionally happen. Don't become discouraged because the person you help may be able to help another and the multiplication of your counseling ministry begins. "With God all things are possible. Only believe."

When counseling, make sure that you are comfortable with your counselee and try to make your counselee feel at ease as much as possible. No one can give or receive counsel effectively when there is uneasiness or tension between the two parties involved.

The counselor MUST NEVER, under any circumstances, disclose any of the information shared by the counselee. This is confidential and must remain confidential at all times. If confidentiality is breached and trust betrayed the counselee will be devastated and may never receive the help needed to get beyond the present problem to live a victorious and productive life.

Pastor, Christian worker, you must RISE TO THIS IMPORTANT CHALLENGE to be able to help people to be over-comers in all areas of their life. Be that person that someone can lean on or talk with when they are lonely, hurt, etc. The Bible states that we are to "bear one another's burdens and fulfill the law of Christ," Galatians 6:2. That means to be there for someone when they need your help. Do not be like the priest and the Levite who saw a man beaten, robbed, and left half dead by thieves but walked by on the other side of the road because they did not want to get involved. Luke 10:31, 32, "And by chance there came down a certain priest that way: and when he saw him, he passed by on the other side. Likewise a Levite, when he was at the place, came and looked on him, and passed by on the other side." My reader friend, God wants us to have the attitude and compassion of the Samaritan who came down that same road and helped this poor man out of his helplessness and misery. This is genuine compassion. Note what Jesus said he did, "....: and when he saw him, he had compassion on him, and went to him, and bound (bandaged) up his wounds, pouring in oil and wine, and set him on his own beast, and brought him to an inn, and took care of him. And on the morrow (the next day) when he departed, he took out two pence (Gr. Denarii), and gave them to the host (innkeeper), and said unto him, Take care of him; and whatsoever thou spendest more, when I come again, I will repay thee" (Luke 10:33-35. The compassion that is needed to do effective counsel is that which will go the extra mile to help the person in need. This is what we see from the story just related and unless we have this compassion we will not do justice to any form of ministry, because there is a certain amount of counseling to be done in all forms of ministry, whether it is teaching a Sunday school class, leading youth services, ministry to seniors, street ministry, etc. Without the compassion of Christ we need to get out of ministry and pray until we are endued with the power of the Holy Spirit, the love of God, and the compassion of Christ to do that which we are called to do as children of the Lord—that is, helping people.

RISE TO THE CHALLENGE, get involved, people are hurting and need help. It is not only a challenge, it is a responsibility and duty for you to help those with problems get the help they need and deserve. Will you be that person, that good Samaritan, who will reach out with arms of love and mercy to help your neighbor? Do it for the cause of Christ and you will receive satisfaction in knowing that you were instrumental in helping a hurting person carry their burden to the Lord.

Are you ready to **RISE TO THE CHALLENGE** OF COUNSELING? If you are and you're not sure how to start, contact me. I will put you in touch with a good school where you will receive the best training possible for the task. Also, there are many excellent books available at the Christian Book Store on the subject of counseling which would be of invaluable help to you.

BIBLIOGRAPHY

Liberty Bible Commentary — Copyright 1982, OTGH, Thomas Nelson Publishers

World's Bible Dictionary

Twentieth Century Bible Dictionary

Modern Globe Dictionary

Funk and Wagnalls Dictionary

The Oxford Pocket Dictionary

Baker's Dictionary of Practical Theology

W. E. Vine's Expository Dictionary of New Testament Words

Foundations of Pentecostal Theology — Life Bible College

Matthew Henry Commentary

The Grimm-Thayer Lexicon

The Minister's Service Manual — Pathway Press, Cleveland, TN.

Jesus, The Master Teacher — Herman Harrell Horne

The Human Situation — W. M. Dixon

Positive Preaching and the Modern Mind — P. T. Forsyth Eaton & Mains, p5f

About the Author

Dr. Terrance Jenkins is a man with a passion for souls and a desire to see men and women equipped to serve the body of Christ. Called of God at age twelve, he answered that call at age eighteen, and began an extensive program of study and training for ministry.

Dr. Jenkins graduated from Canada Christian College, Toronto,Ontario, Canada with three theological degrees (Associate, Bachelor and Master of Theological Studies.) He later had conferred upon him the 'Honorary' Doctor of Divinity degree by Dallas Faith Clinic in conjunction with Kingsway Bible College and Seminary, Des Moins, Iowa. In 1991 Dr. Jenkins earned a Doctor of Theology degree at International Bible College and Seminary, Independence, MO. His doctoral 'thesis' was "Nineteen Special Gifts of God To His Children." In 1995 Dr. Jenkins was commissioned as a Certified Pastoral Counselor by the Evangelical Order of Certified Pastoral Counselors of America and in 1998 was ordained as a Psycho-therapist and Counsellor by the same organization.

Dr. Jenkins has served on various denominational boards and committees and is past president and CEO of National Native Bible College in Ontario, Canada.

He has traveled extensively throughout the United States and Canada, has preached at several minister's conventions and conferences, as well as plant three churches in Canada.

CPSIA information can be obtained at www.ICGtesting.com
Printed in the USA

267865BV00001B/12/P